Chords and Tunings for Fretted Instruments

by Larry Sandberg

Order No. OK 63412
International Standard Book Number: 0.8256.0198.3
Library of Congress Catalog Card Number: 77-82817

Exclusive Distributors:
Music Sales Corporation
257 Park Avenue South, New York, NY 10010 USA
Music Sales Limited
8/9 Frith Street, London W1V 5TZ England
Music Sales Pty. Limited
120 Rothschild Street, Rosebery, Sydney, NSW 2018, Australia

Printed in the United States of America by
Vicks Lithograph and Printing Corporation

Contents

Introduction

This book is intended as a one-stop chord guide for folk, bluegrass, contemporary pop, blues and rock music. The chords shown have been carefully selected on pragmatic and realistic grounds in order to offer the most useful, reasonable, and best-sounding alternatives in most typically imaginable situations, with a few extra chord forms thrown in just in case.

The more chords you know, and the more different shapes for the same chord, the more varied and interesting your playing will become. The most obvious use for this book is as an emergency reference guide for the time that you're learning a new song and need a chord or a tuning that you don't know. But you can also use this book experimentally. Nothing will improve your playing so much as the imaginative efforts you yourself bring to bear. Take it upon yourself to learn a new chord now and then, and assimilate it into your playing. Learn new ways of playing chords, in different positions on the fingerboard. Or try some basic chord substitutions: C9 instead of C7 for a jazzy sound, or likewise Am7 instead of an Am. Or CM7 or C6 instead of a plain major chord, for an open, dreamy sound. Your ear will tell you when these substitutions work and when they don't, and you'll be able to add a new range of colors and emotions to your playing.

The Chromatic Scale

The chromatic scale consists simply of the names of all the notes, fret by fret. Knowing it is roughly equivalent to knowing the points of the compass, and in order to use it you don't have to know the more complicated aspects of music theory any more than you have to know the principles of electromagnetic force in order to find directions. Starting with the letter A, since it's the first letter of the 7-letter musical alphabet, the names of the 12 notes in our musical system are:

A	A♯/B♭	B	C	C♯/D♭	D	D♯/E♭	E	F	F♯/G♭	G	G♯/A♭	A	A♯/B♭	B	etc
1	2	3	4	5	6	7	8	9	10	11	12	1	2 etc.		

After the 12th note, the series starts all over again. It's important to understand that A♯/B♭, etc, are two different names for the same sound. The distance of two frets is called a tone.

Once you know the chromatic scale, you can move notes and chords all over the fingerboard. For example, the note on the first fret of an open D string is called D♯ or E♭, the note on the second fret E, etc. A D chord moved one fret higher on the fingerboard becomes a D♯ or E♭ chord, an Am chord moved two frets higher becomes a Bm chord, and so on.

Types of Chords, Symbols, and Abbreviations

Here is a list of chord-types, together with the abbreviations found in common use. The chords based on C are given as an example, but the equivalent relationships apply in all keys.

C (C△)	C major C-E-G
CM7 (C Maj 7, C△7, C7)	C major seventh C-E-G-B
CM9 (C Maj 9, C△9)	C major ninth C-E-G-B-D
C6	C (major) sixth C-E-G-A
C6/9 (C9/6)	C sixth, add ninth C-E-G-D-A
Cm (Cmin, C-)	C minor C-E♭-G
Cm7 (Cmin7, C-7)	C minor seventh C-E♭-G-B♭
Cm6 (Cmin6, C-6)	C minor sixth C-E♭-G-A
Cm9 (Cmin9, C-9)	C minor ninth C-E♭-G-B♭-D
Cm7♭5 (Cmin7 5, C-7-5, Cø)	C minor seventh flat fifth C-E♭-G♭-B♭
C7	C seventh, (C dominant seventh) C-E-G-B♭
C7sus4	C seventh suspended fourth C-F-G-B♭
C9	C ninth (C dominant ninth) C-E-G-B♭-D
C7♭5 (C7-5)	C seventh flat fifth C-E-G♭-B♭
C7♭9 (C7-9)	C seventh flat ninth C-E-G-B♭-D♭
C7♯9 (C7+9)	C seventh sharp ninth C-E-G-B♭-D♯
C11	for practical purposes = C7sus4
C13	C thirteenth C-E-G-B♭-(D)-A
C⁰ (Cdim, C-)	C diminished C-E♭-G♭. For practical purposes, this chord does not exist in folk, pop, and jazz music. When you see this symbol, it is shorthand for C⁰7.
C⁰7 (Cdim7, C-7)	C diminished seventh. C-E♭-G♭-B♭♭ (=C-E♭-G♭-A)
C+ (Caug)	C augmented C-E-G♯
C+7 (C7+, Caug7)	C augmented seventh, C seventh augmented C-E-G♯-B♭

Be careful to note that different editors and arrangers might use the minus sign (-) to mean either minor or diminished. Your own best bet to avoid confusion is to use one of the other abbreviations instead. If you're learning a song and don't know what the editor means, try minor first, since minor chords are more common. But you might have to try both minor and diminished to see which sounds right.

It is difficult or even physically impossible to play several of the more complicated chords in a complete form on the guitar. This is even more true for the banjo and mandolin, both with fewer strings. Therefore, technically "incomplete" forms are occasionally given.

6 5 4 3 2 1   or   4 3 2 1

←→ Frets
↕ Strings

( ) = Optional note
o = Open string may be played
× = Do not play open string

5

Chords for Piano, Organ and Accordion

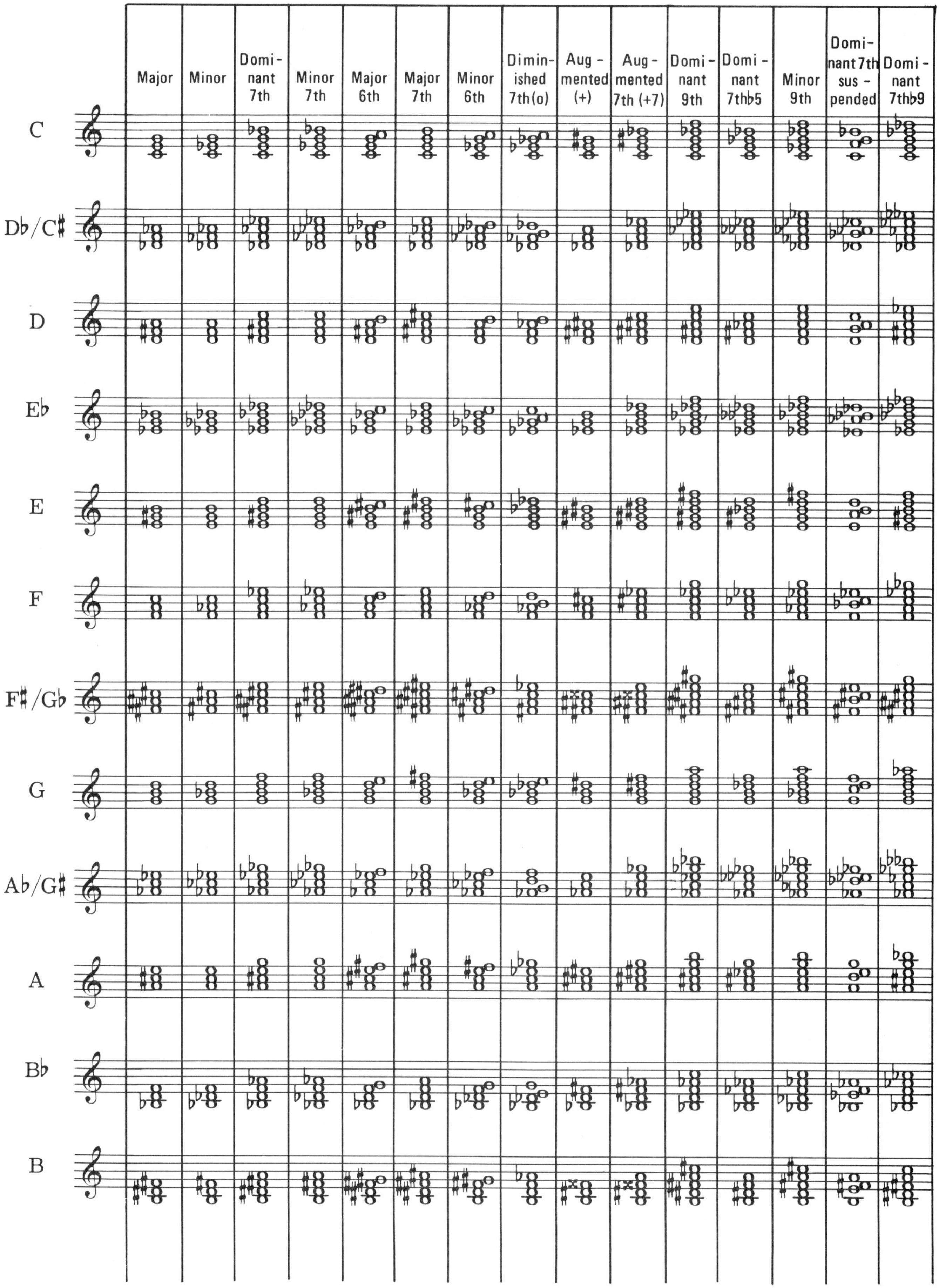

Standard Tuning for Guitar, 12-String Guitar, Bass, Ukelele, Baritone Ukelele, and Tenor Guitar

The six-string guitar used for folk, blues, jazz, classical and flamenco music is tuned:

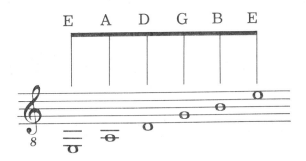

The 12-string guitar is essentially a six-string guitar with six pairs of strings, the lowest four of which are tuned in octaves, the highest two in unison:*

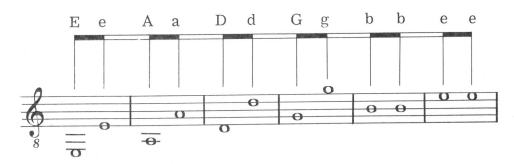

The ukelele is tuned in the same relationship as the first four strings of the guitar—but all the strings are higher. The first three strings are five tones higher; the fourth string is an octave and a fifth higher. For practical purposes, this means that the first (highest) four strings' worth of the chord diagrams in this section may be used for the ukelele, but the chords must be renamed according to the following transposition chart:

GUITAR	=	UKELELE
C	=	G
C#/Db	=	G#/Ab
D	=	A
D#/Eb	=	A#/Bb
E	=	B
F	=	C
F#/Gb	=	C#/Db
G	=	D
G#/Ab	=	D#/Eb
A	=	E
A#/Bb	=	F
B	=	F#/Gb

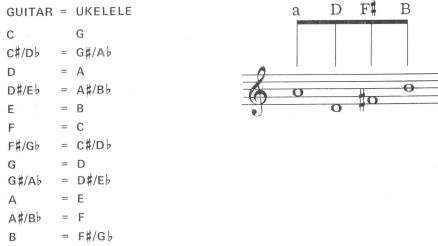

The baritone ukelele is tuned like the first four strings of the guitar, and so the first four strings of the chord diagrams in this section may be used without transposition.

*Though most newer 12-strings can be tuned up to pitch—with sufficiently light strings—many guitarists prefer to keep their instruments tuned 1 step (2 frets) lower: DD GG CC FF AA DD.

The tenor guitar may be tuned like the first four strings of the guitar, but a fourth higher. Therefore, the first four strings of the diagrams in this section may be used, but the chords must be renamed according to the following transposition chart:

GUITAR = TENOR GUITAR

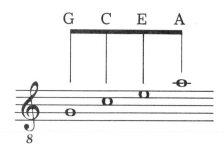

C	=	F
C♯/D♭	=	F♯/G♭
D	=	G♭
D♯/E♭	=	G♯/A♭
E	=	A
F	=	A♯/B♭
F♯/G♭	=	B
G	=	C
G♯/A♭	=	C♯/D♭
A	=	D
A♯/B♭	=	D♯/E♭
B	=	E

The tenor guitar may also be tuned like the first four strings of a standard guitar, a fifth higher than a standard guitar (use the ukelele transposition chart) or like a tenor banjo (use the chords in the mandolin/tenor banjo section).

The bass and electric bass are tuned like the lowest four strings of the guitar, but two octaves lower. Full chords are not customarily played on the bass, but the diagrams in this section may be used to help figure out harmony combinations and the fingerings of arpeggios (chords played one note at a time).

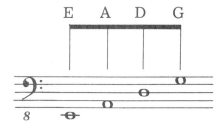

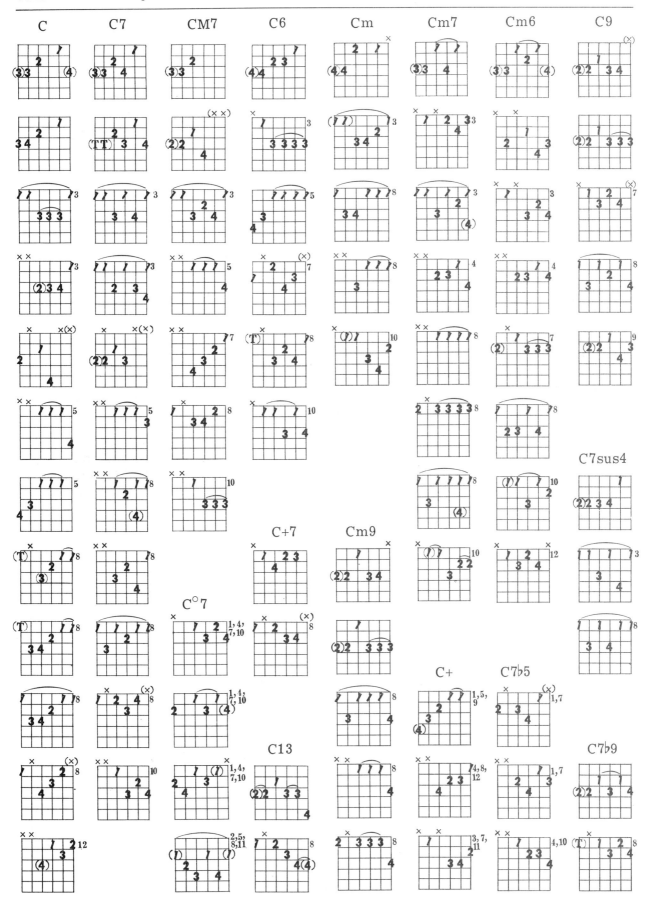

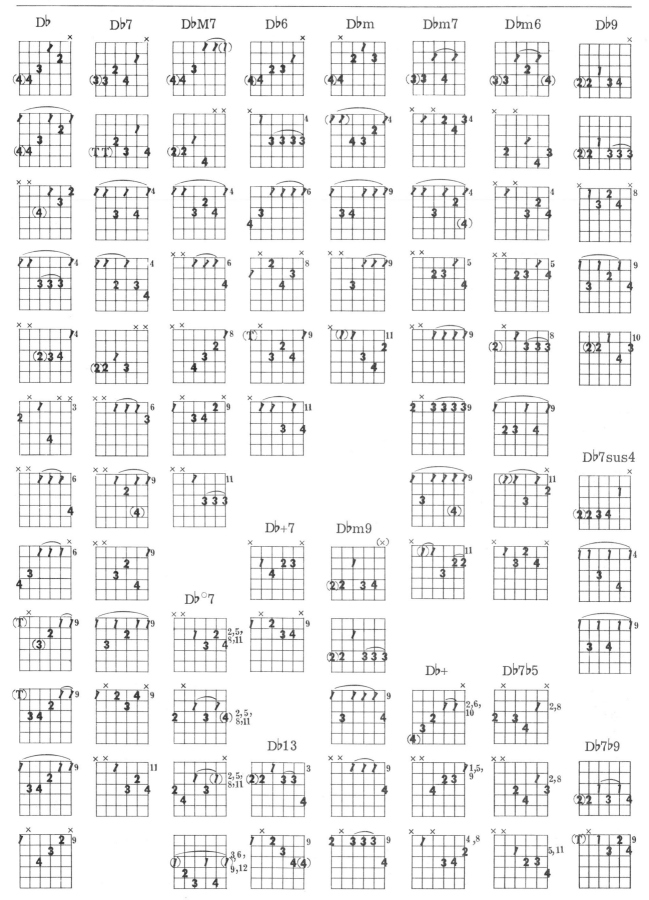

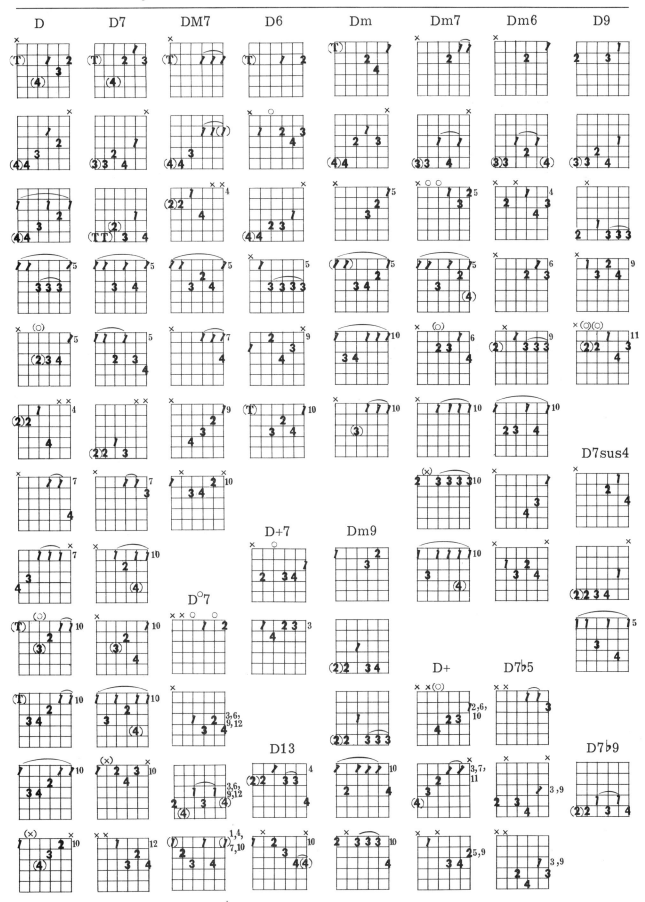

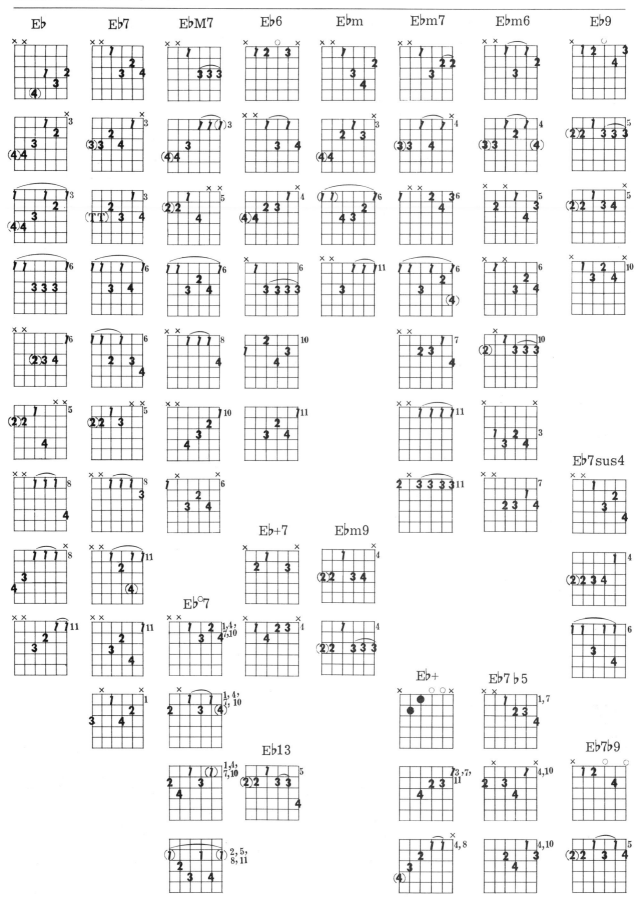

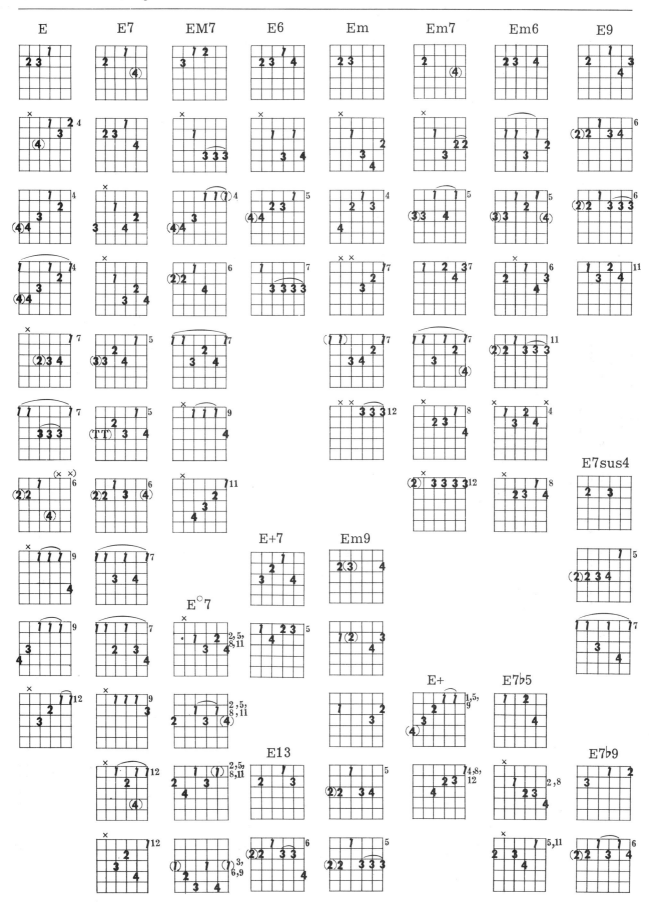

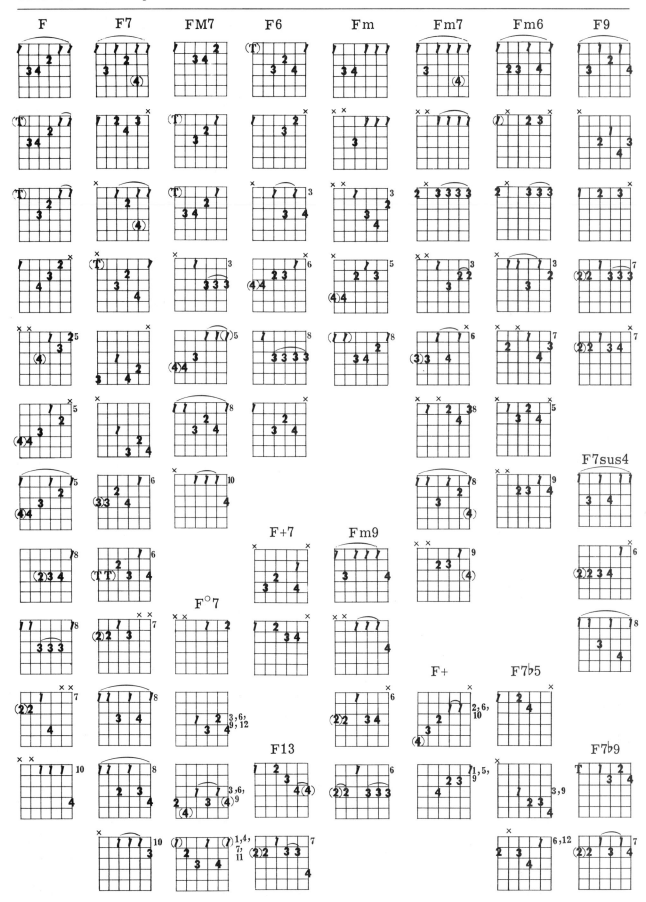

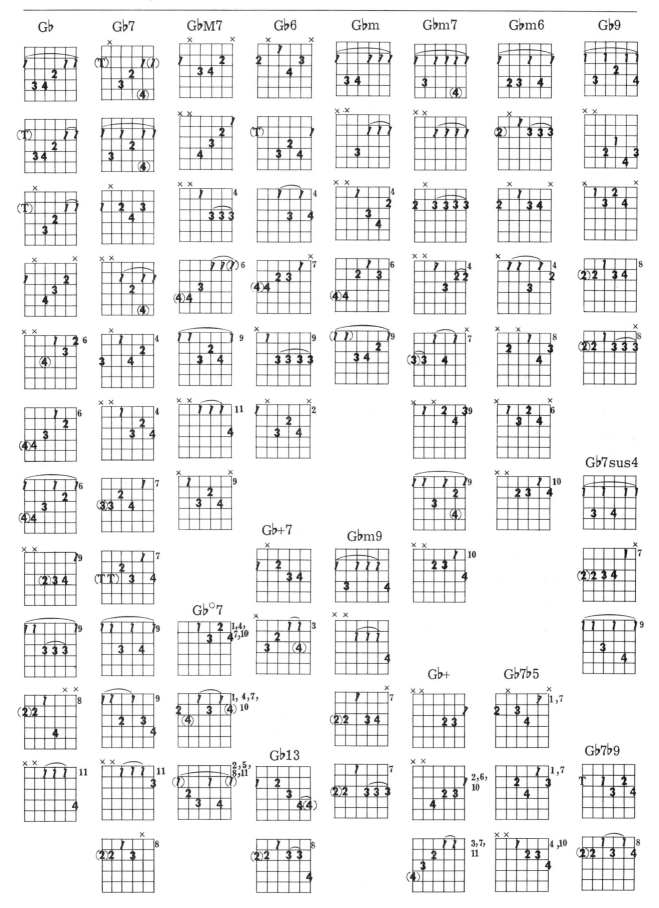

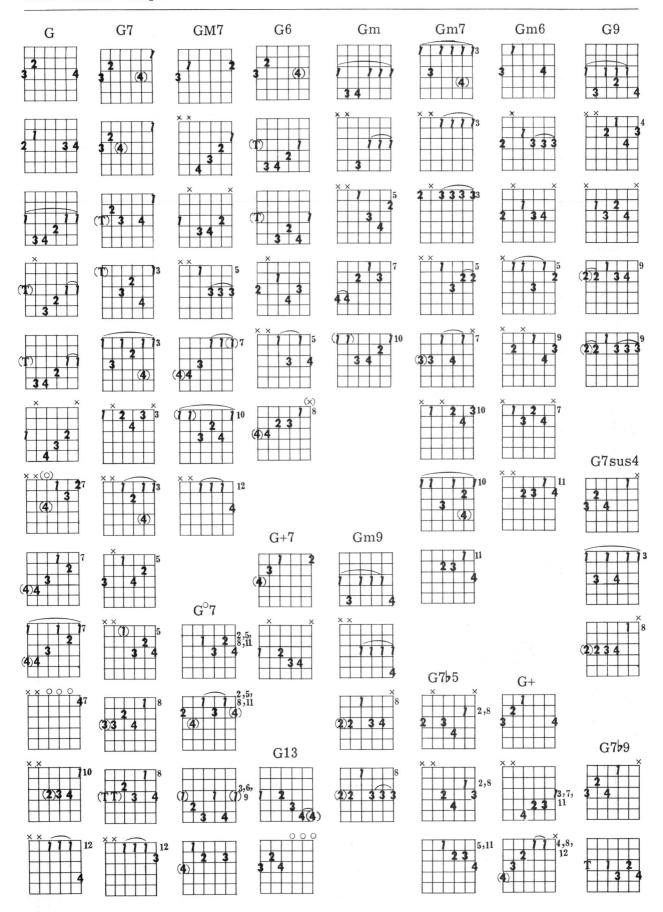

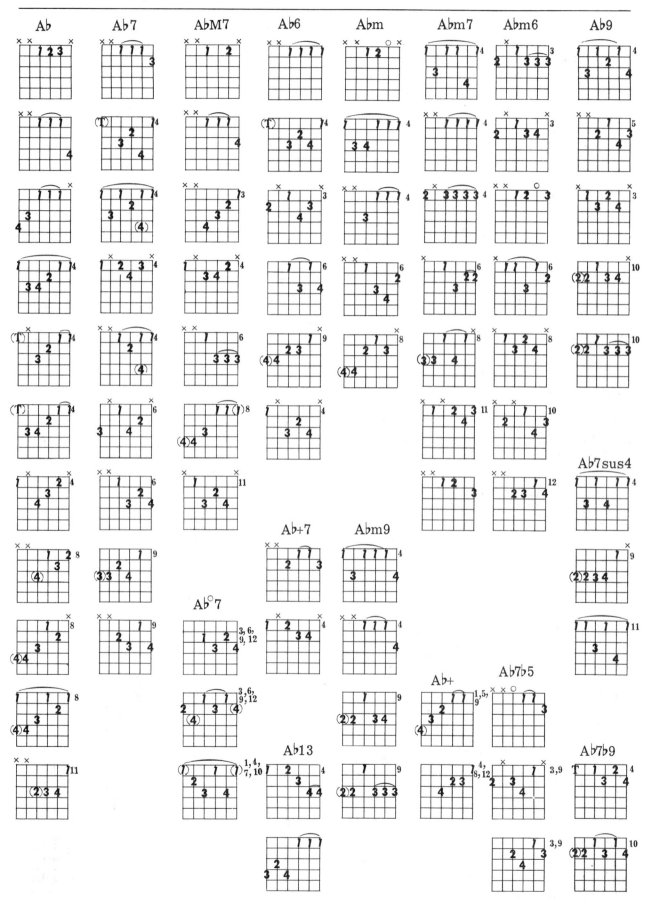

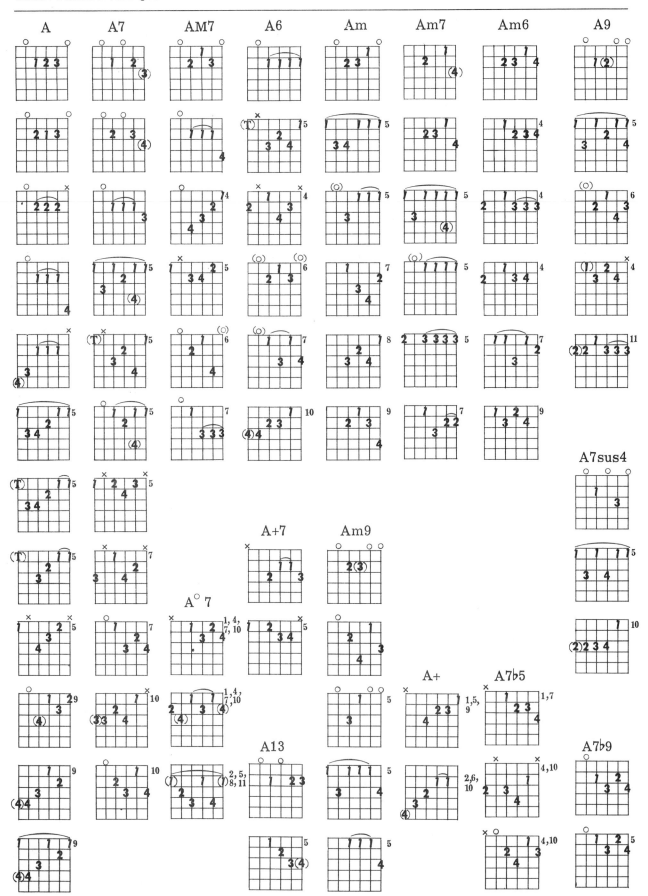

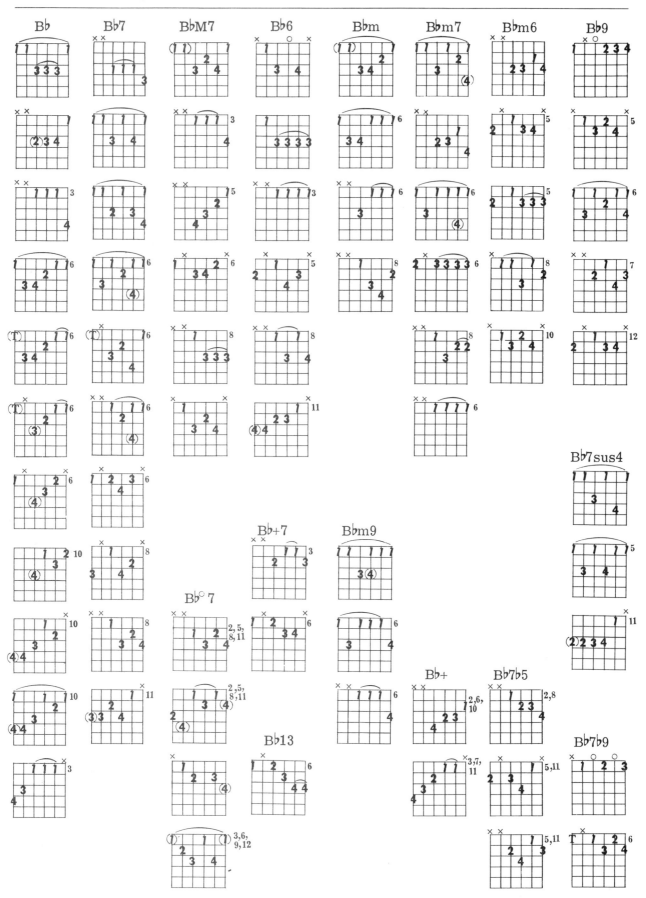

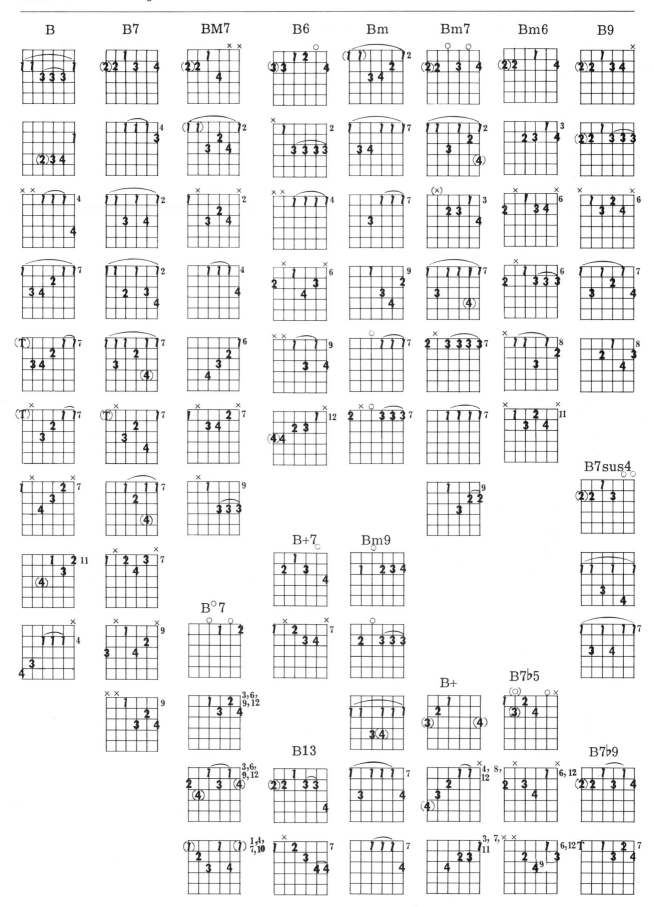

Here are a few more chord forms, rarely used. They are given in C, but they can be moved anywhere on the fingerboard, where their names can be found by using the chromatic scale. (see *Introduction.*)

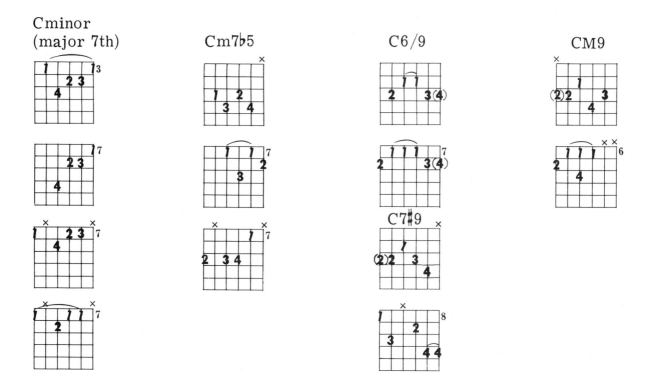

Modal Guitar Chords

Exciting contemporary sounds can be produced in modal playing, where chords are constructed out of nontraditional intervals using any tone of the scale. Modal chords aren't necessarily given names, since the traditional system of naming chords just falls aprart in this context. The following selection of chords is offered by way of introduction to this intriguing sound. They are constructed in the Dorian mode of E (scale: E, F♯, G, A, B, C♯, D, E).

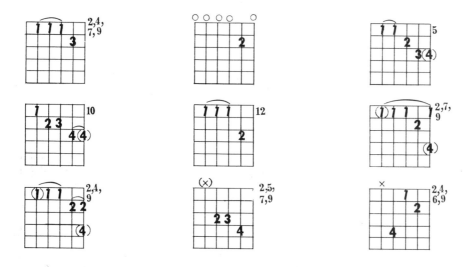

Open Tunings for Guitar

An open tuning is one in which the guitar is so tuned that a complete chord is produced by the open strings. Open tunings offer a variety of musical possibilities that would be difficult or impossible to obtain in standard tuning: unusual chord sounds against open drone strings, easy access to the whole fingerboard with a slide or bottleneck, and so on. In addition, many guitarists find that working in a new tuning breaks their old habits, and causes them to approach the instrument with fresh insights and new ideas.

As a rule, the guitar in open tuning is played in the key of which the open chord is the tonic.

**Guitar: G Tuning
(DGDGBD)**

In this tuning the guitar is tuned to an open G chord:

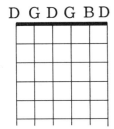
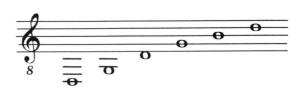

This versatile tuning corresponds to G tuning on the banjo. Occasionally it is used as an A tuning, with each string tuned one tone higher so that an open A chord results. In this case, the chords in the following diagrams should be named one tone higher (G becomes A, C7 becomes D7, etc.).

People often call this tuning "Spanish" tuning.

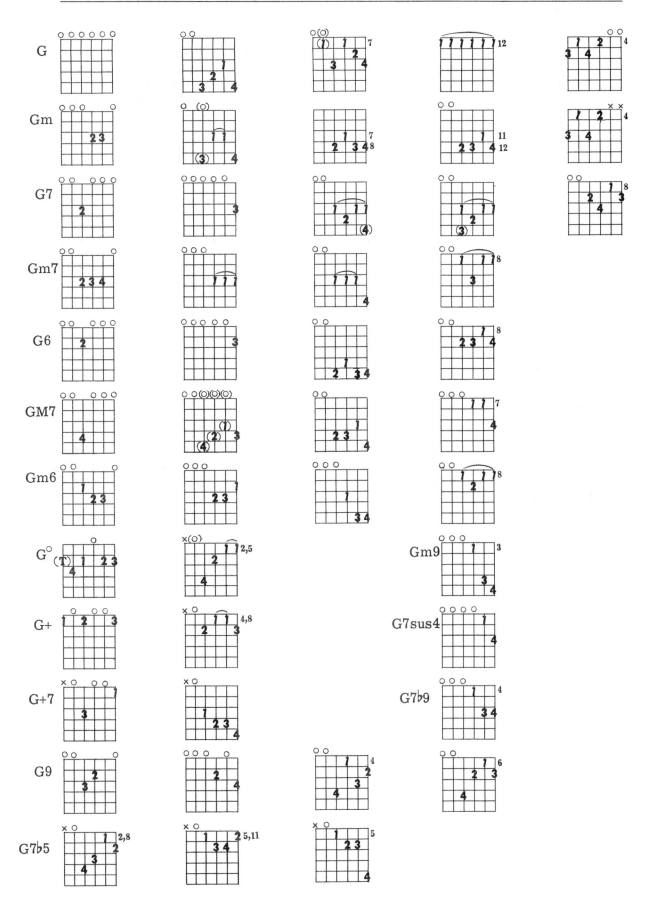

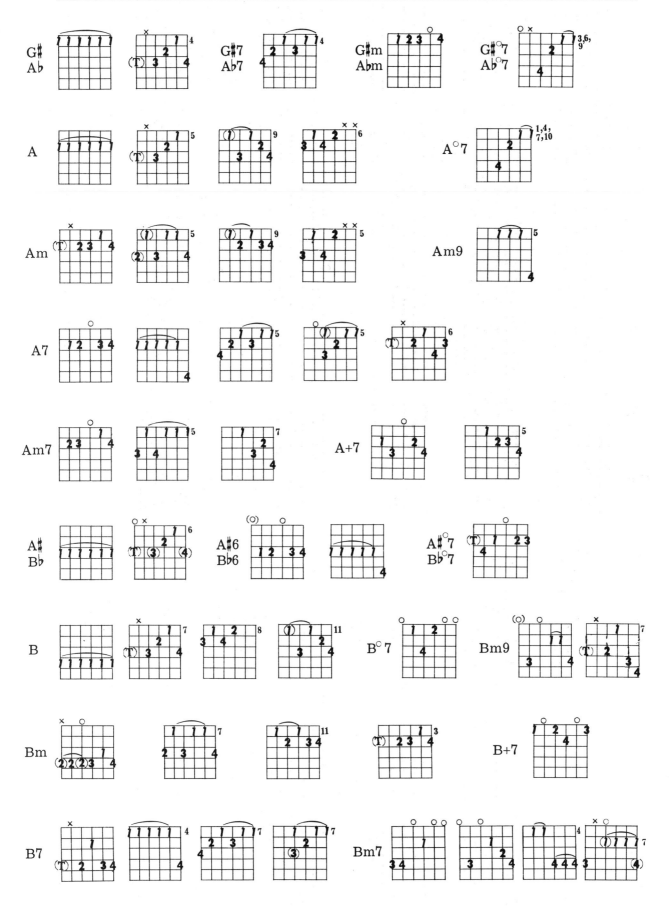

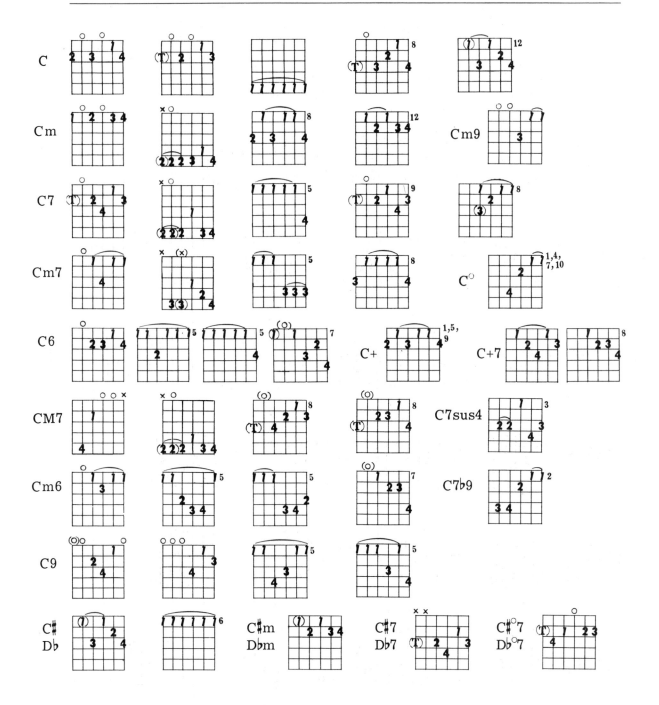

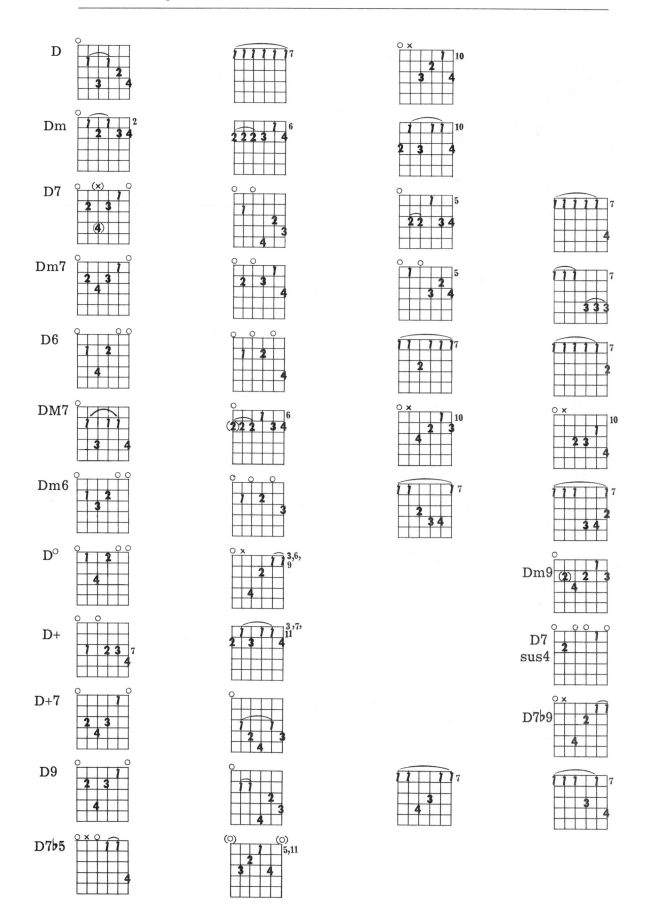

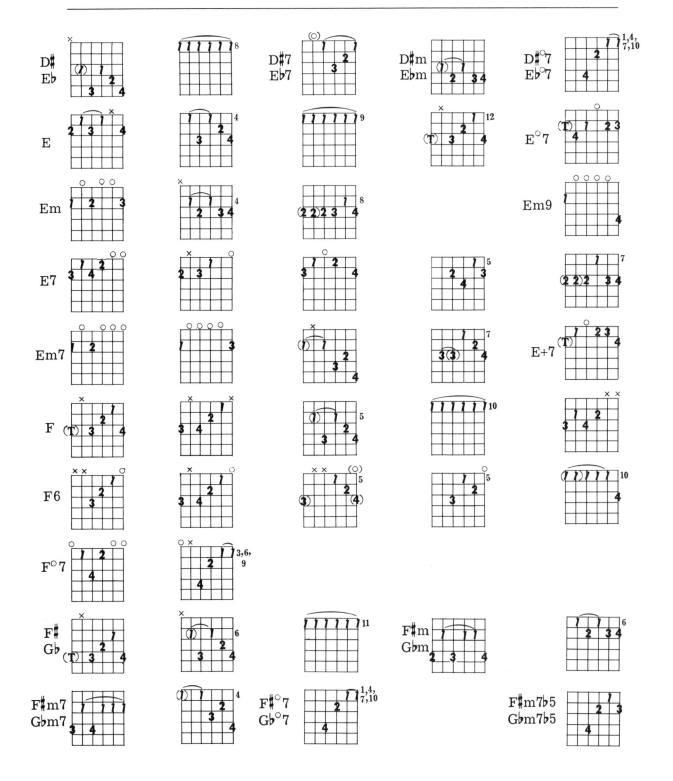

Guitar: D Tuning
(DADF♯AD)

This is also known as "slack key", "Hawaiian", and "Vastopol" tuning, the last after a parlor guitar piece called "Sevastopol" that was popular in the early part of this century. The guitar is tuned to an open D major chord:

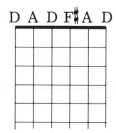

Open D is probably the most versatile of tunings, lending itself to just about any sort of song in any style, including slide and lap-steel styles.

Some players prefer to tune their instruments to an open E chord (EAEG♯BE) with each string one tone higher than in D tuning. This produces a brighter sound, since the strings are tighter, but it may be rough on your strings and on the neck of your guitar. If you use E instead of D, name the chords on the diagrams that follow one tone higher (e.g. D becomes E, A7 becomes B7, etc.)

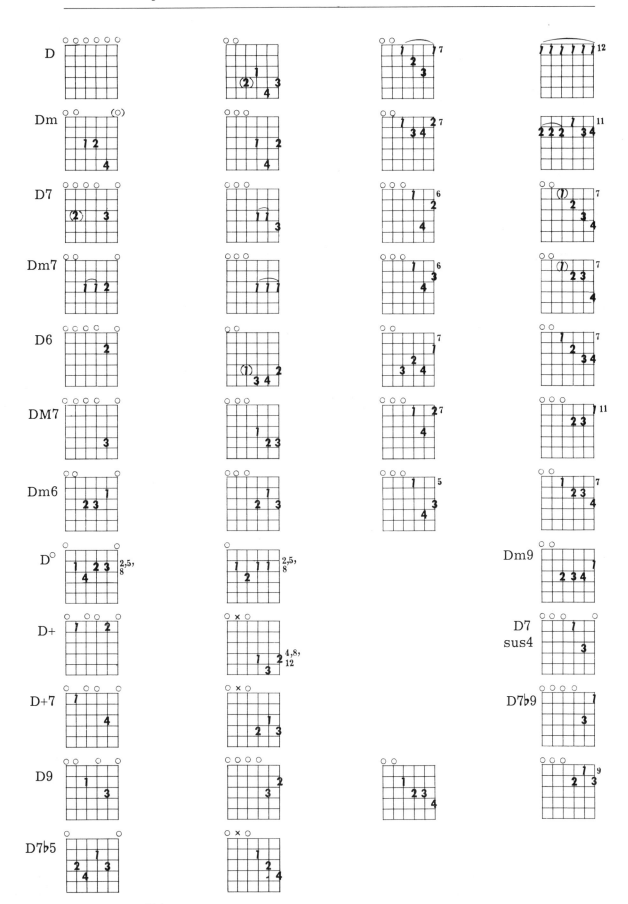

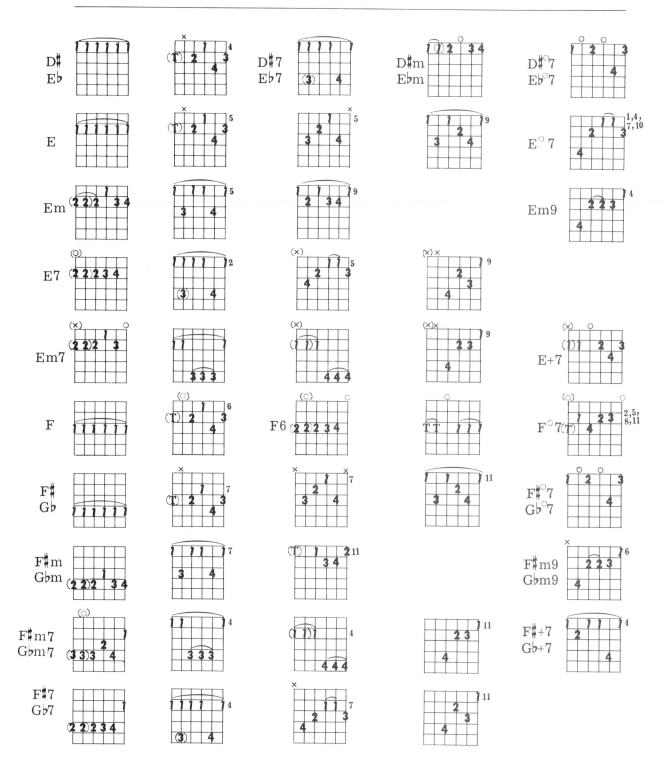

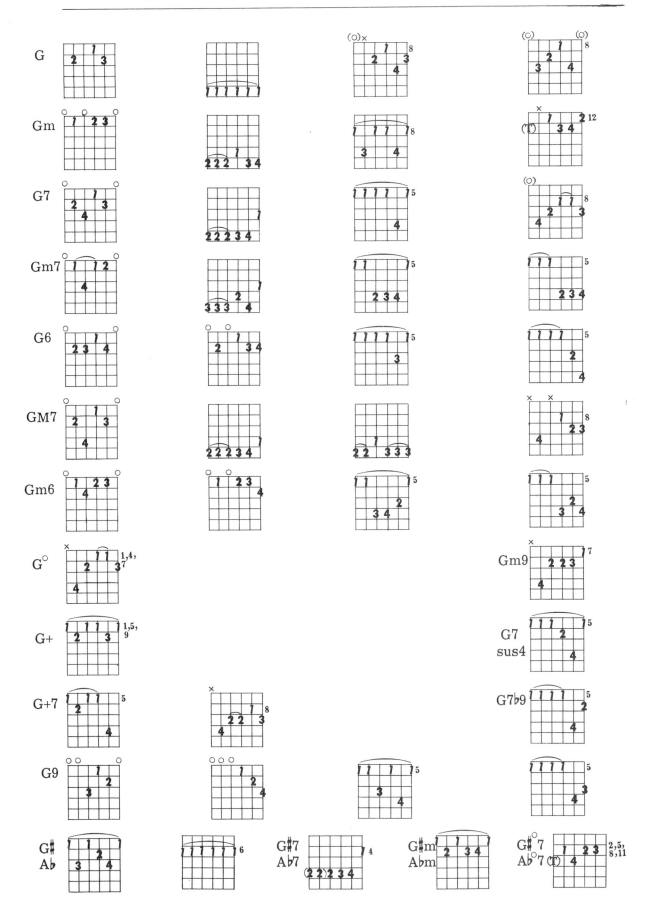

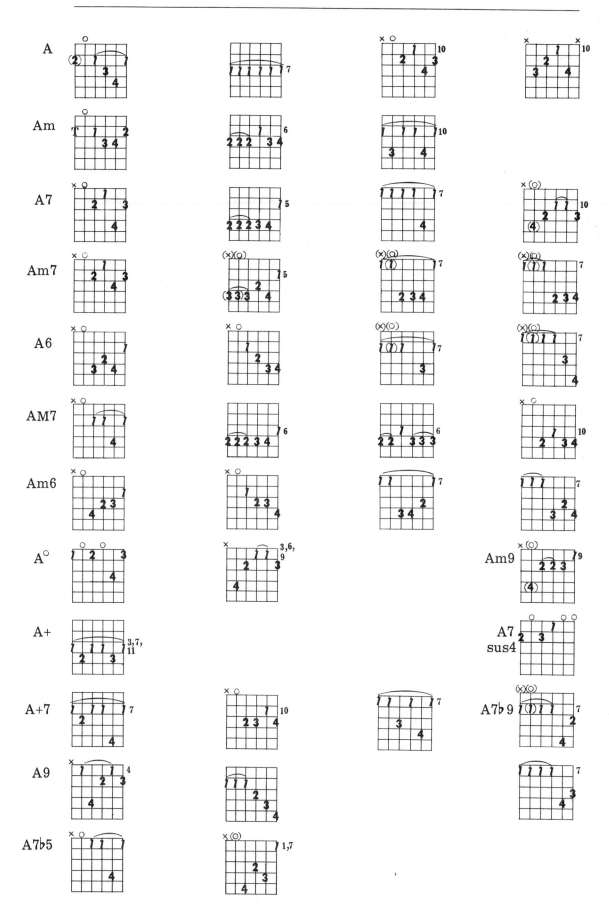

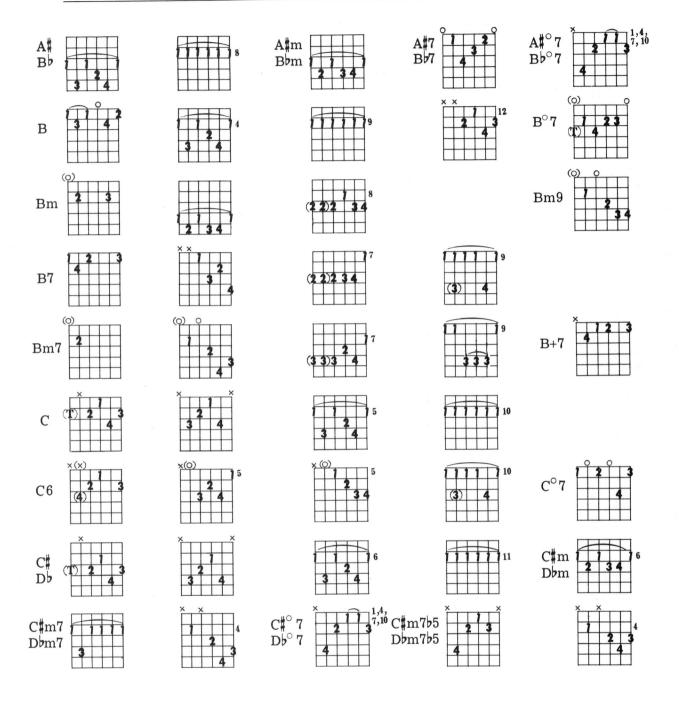

Guitar: D Modal Tuning
(DADGAD)

In this tuning the guitar is tuned to a D chord with a suspended fourth and without a third. The resulting sound is not quite definable as either minor or major, and it provides a striking texture at once very modern and very archaic. This tuning is rarely used by traditional guitarists, but is favored by modern guitarists especially for bluesy sounds with very simple chord changes.

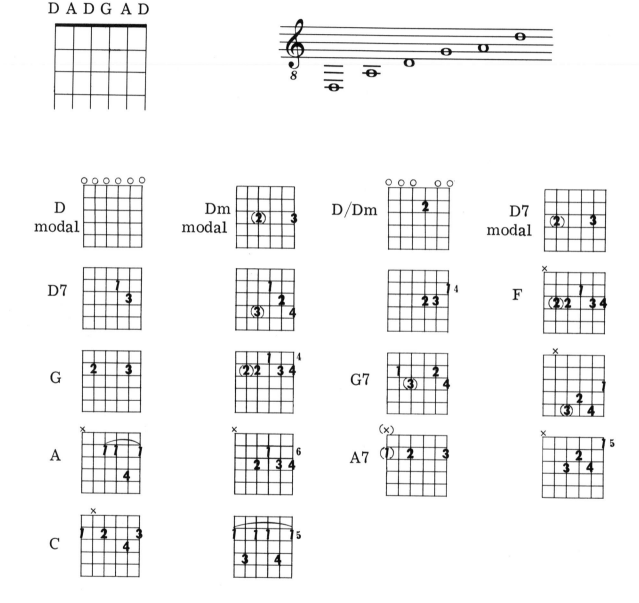

Guitar: Dropped D Tuning
(DADGBE)

D A D G B E

 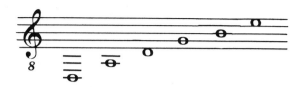

This is the same as standard tuning, with the sixth string dropped one whole tone to D in order to facilitate playing in the key of D, particularly in fingerpicking style where an alternating bass note pattern is called for. You can use any chord shape from standard tuning as long as you leave out the sixth string. In addition, you can work out new fingerings by compensating for the two-fret drop of the sixth string. The fingerings below are in common use:

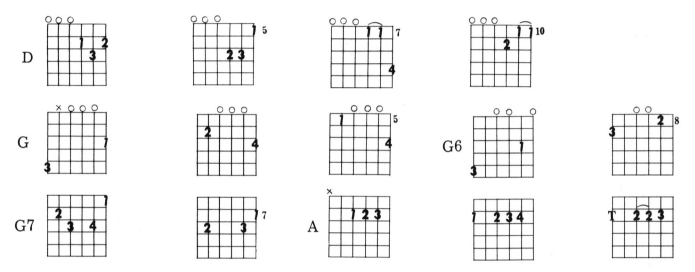

Guitar: D Minor "Cross-note" Tuning
(DADFAD)

The guitar is tuned to an open D minor chord, but the actual playing can be done in either D minor or D major.

D A D F A D

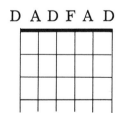 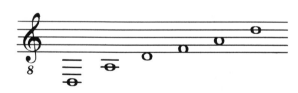

This tuning is called "cross-note" (or sometimes "cross-key") because the old-time bluesmen found it so effective for crossing over between minor and major tonalities. It also serves admirably as a vehicle for minor key songs that don't have the remotest blues feeling about them, and some strikingly modern sounds can be had this way.

Some guitarists (especially the old bluesmen) prefer to tune the strings one tone higher to an open E minor chord: EBEGBE. This might be a bit rough on your strings and neck, but it's much easier to get in and out of the tuning this way, since only the fifth and fourth strings need to be changed from standard tuning.

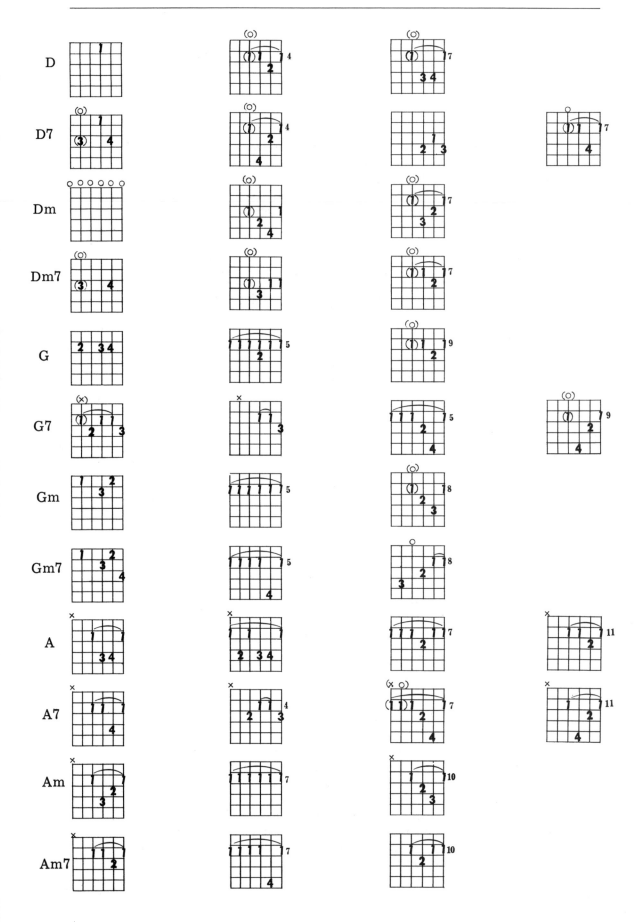

In this tuning, especially useful for a delta blues sound, the guitar is tuned to an open A chord:

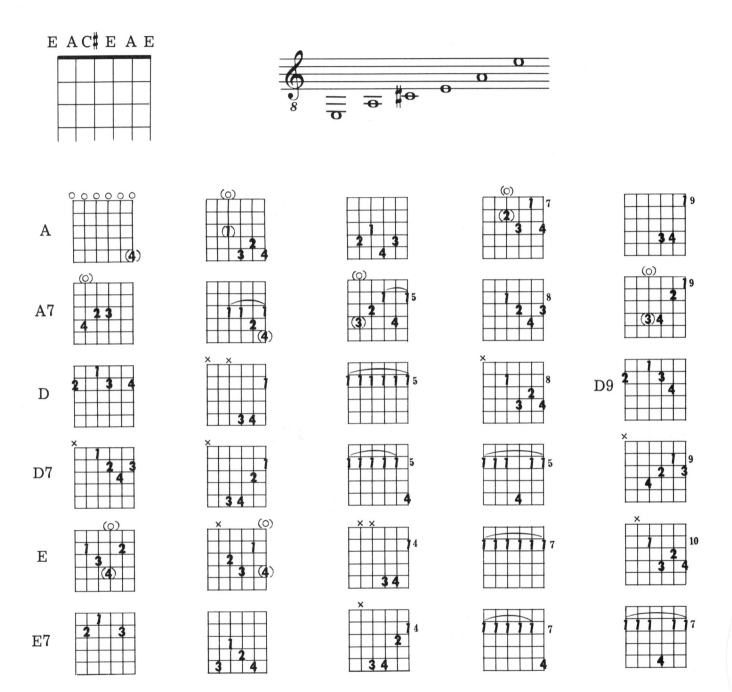

Guitar: C Tuning
(CGCGCE)

A very beautiful tuning not used today as often as formerly. This is surprising, since it represents possibilities for a whole array of sounds from the funkiest of blues to the laciest of filigree ballad accompaniments, from the most archaic to the most modern of sounds. A few of the old-timers I've met use this tuning for pieces that are mostly played today in G and D tunings. The guitar is tuned to an open C chord, corresponding to open C tuning on the banjo:

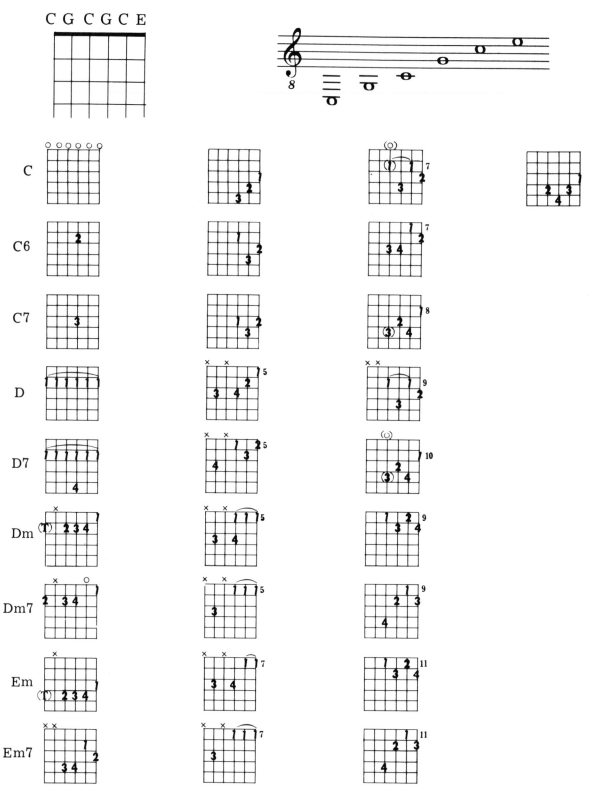

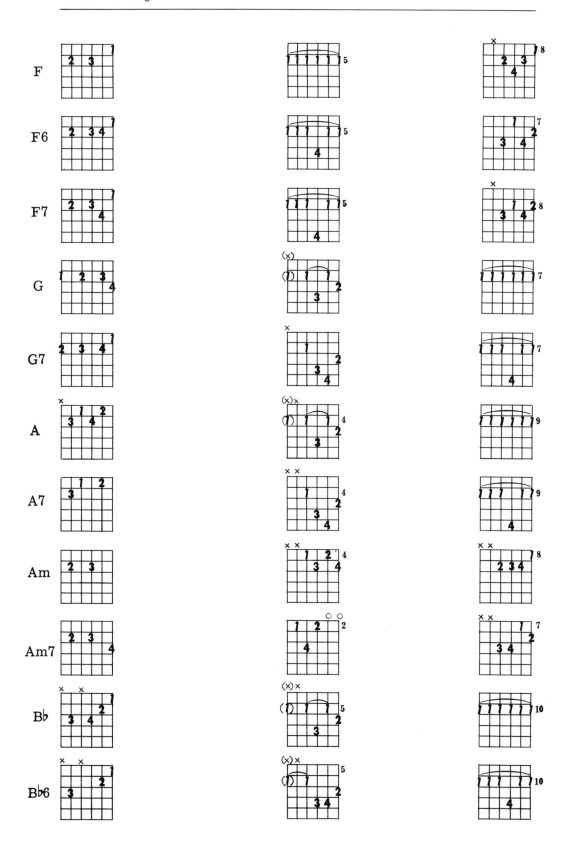

Tunings for Slide Guitar, Lap Steel and Dobro

Although "Dobro" is properly speaking a brand name, the term is used loosely for any guitar, usually with a built-in metal resonator, that is held horizontally on the lap and played with a steel fretting bar (just called a "steel") that in effect constitutes a moveable fret.

In standard bluegrass tuning the dobro is tuned to an open G chord—but not exactly the same G chord as in open G guitar tuning.

G B D G B D

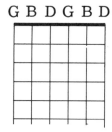

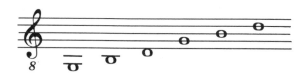

Compare this order of notes GBDGBD
with open G "Spanish" tuning   DGDGBD. The two lowest strings are different, so that bluegrass tuning offers two identical pairs of three strings each. This facilitates visualizing chord shapes when working with the steel. But it's important to note that the highest strings in both tunings are identical.

The dobro can also be tuned in open G "Spanish" tuning and in open D tuning. In addition, there exist seven- and eight-string instruments, for which players like to make up their own tunings usually based on one of the six-string tunings. Here are three sample tunings for a seven- or eight-string instrument:

(D)GBDGBDE for a western swing sound.

(D)GBDGBDF for more bluesy, funky possibilities.

(D)GDEGBDF as a versatile compromise between the two sounds, but requiring extreme care both with the steel and with the righthand picking.

The following diagrams represent not only the rather limited number of full chords available with the steel, but also the various partial-chord harmony combinations that are in general use. Some of these combinations are ambiguous—that is, they may stand for more than one chord. Many require the steel to be held diagonally, which is a difficult art to master. Be sure to pluck only the strings indicated, although the steel may be resting across other strings as well.

These chord shapes will work in both bluegrass and "Spanish" G tunings. For playing in different keys, they may be located in other places up and down the neck according to the chromatic scale (see *Introduction*).

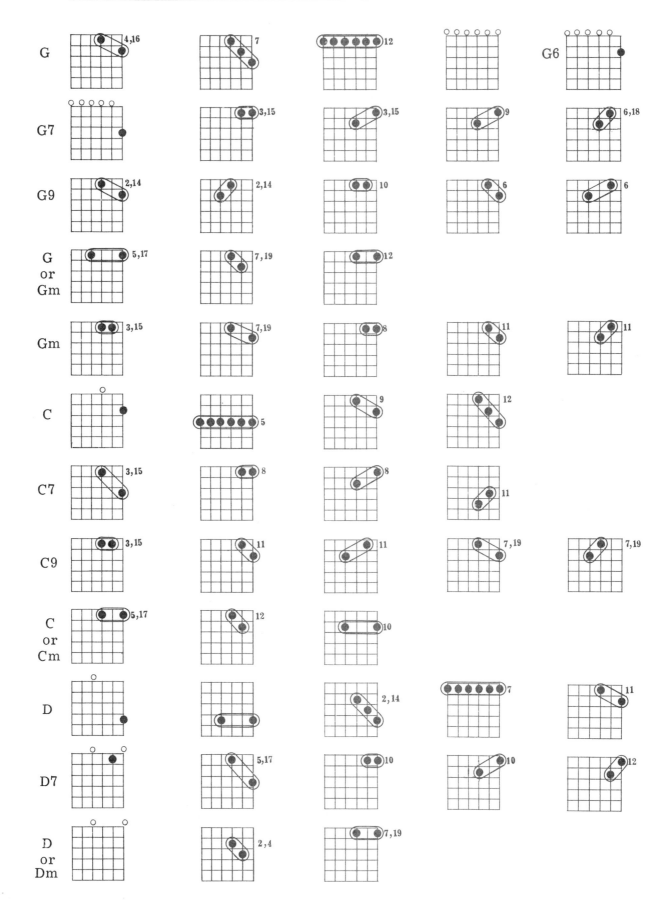

The Five-String Banjo

The five-string banjo is usually tuned to an open chord and played only in that key, or in a very few closely related leys. In order to play in keys for which a tuning does not exist, a capo must be used. A few banjo players prefer to retune all their strings a few frets higher or lower instead of using a capo. When retuning or using a capo, remember to retune the fifth string also. Tuning buttons or a fifth string capo must be added to banjos not so equipped.

Except in rare cases, the high drone fifth string is not fretted, and so may be dissonant with the chords that are being played. This quality gives the banjo its characteristic charm, but in cases of extreme dissonance the fifth string must be omitted.

Many banjo players learn a great number of tunings, sometimes using a whole new tuning just for one special piece. You can find a list of 67 tunings for the five-string banjo in the *Folk Music Sourcebook* by Larry Sandberg and Dick Weissman.

Banjo: G Tuning
(GDGBD)

In this tuning the banjo is tuned to an open G chord:

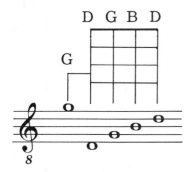

This is the standard tuning for bluegrass and for most folk and contemporary music as well, and is the tuning it makes most sense to learn first. Mostly it's used for playing in the key of G, but of all tunings it offers the greatest potential for playing in other keys as well. It is particularly well suited for playing in the keys of A minor (with the fifth string tuned to A) and E minor (with the fifth string tuned to E). The key of D (fifth string tuned to A or F♯), the key of C (fifth string tuned to G) and the key of F (fifth string tuned to F) are also easily accessible. In addition, these fifth-string tuning variations can also be used to lend an exotic quality to some tunes in the key of G.

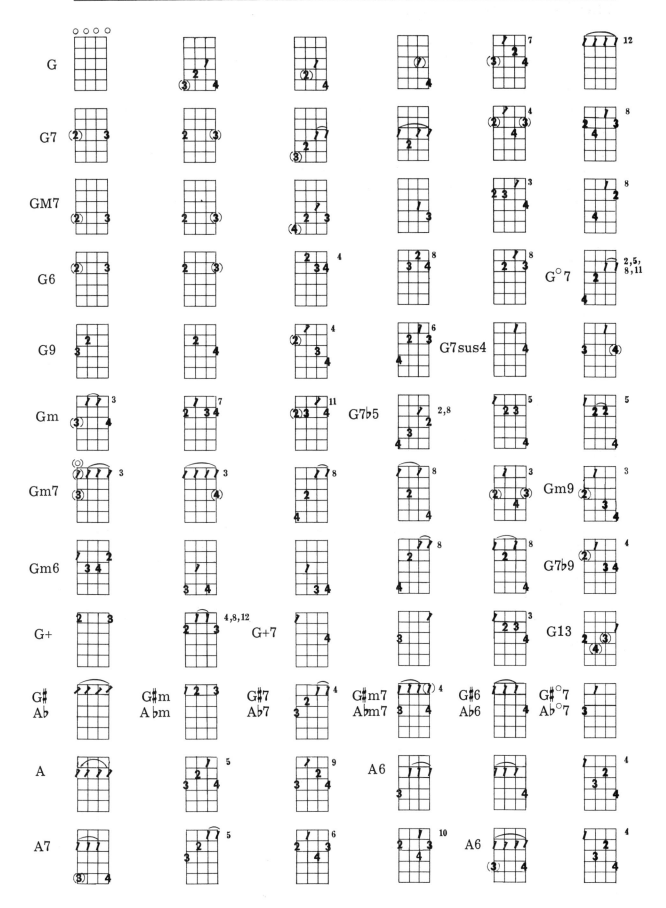

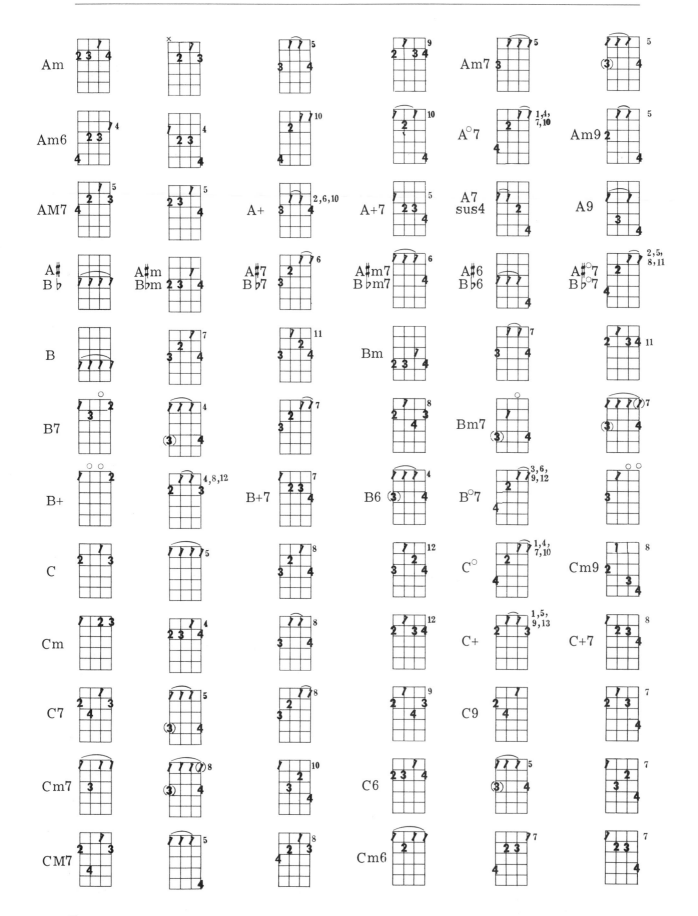

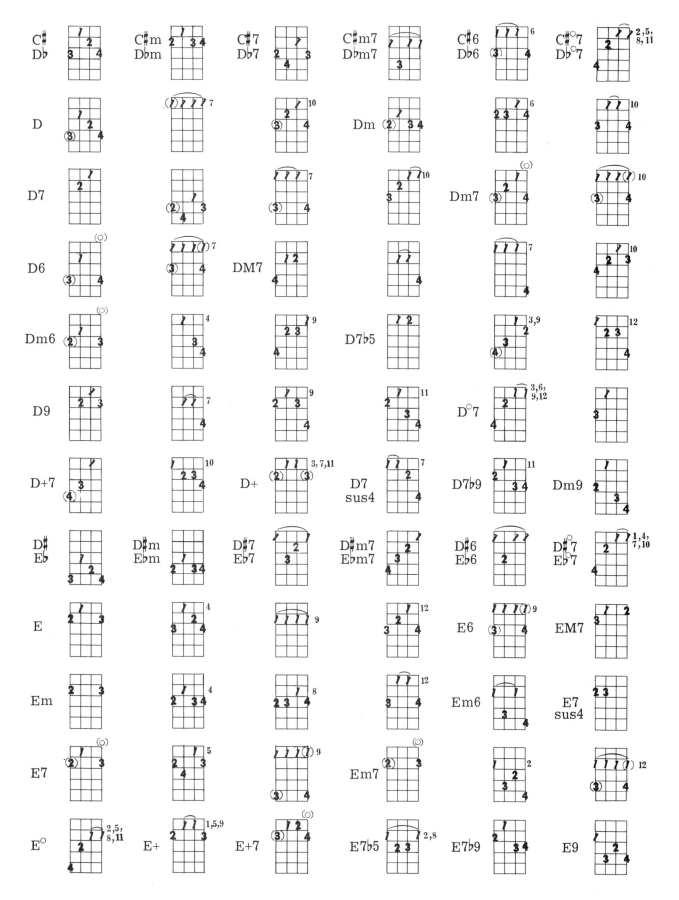

45

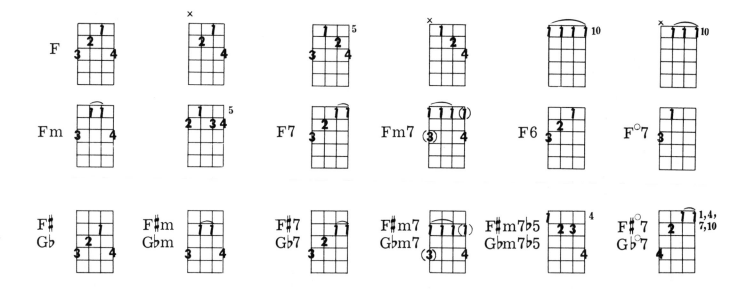

Banjo G Minor Tuning
(GDGB♭D)

In this tuning the strings are tuned to an open G minor chord:

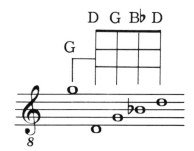

G minor is an especially effective tuning for ballads that have a high range, and for tunes where the archaic sound quality of the more frequently used G modal tuning is not desirable. It has been rarely used by mountain and traditional bluegrass musicians, but it's extremely common among city and newgrass musicians, especially for adapting contemporary material for the banjo.

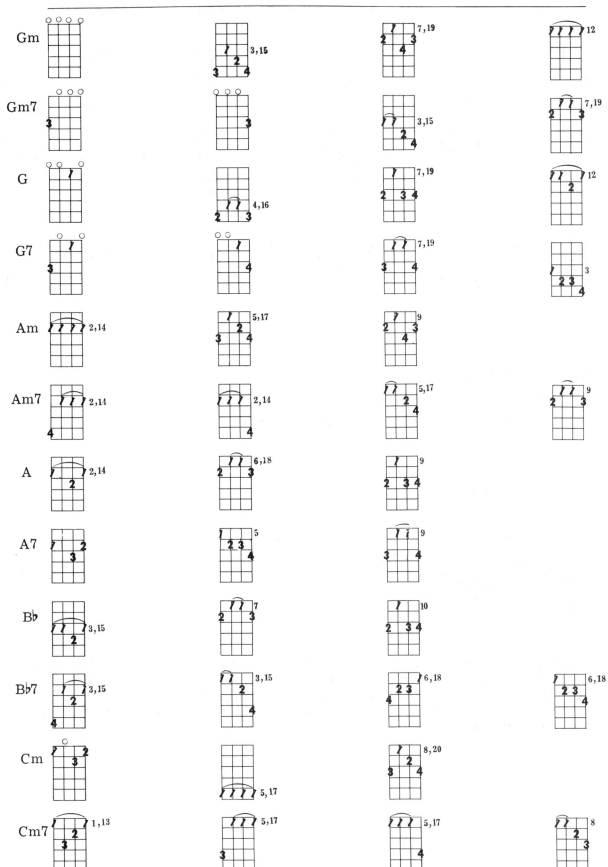

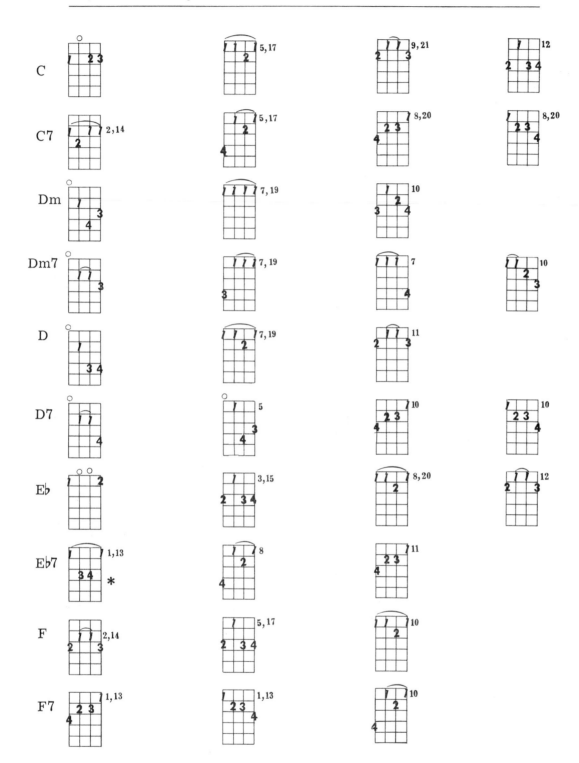

Banjo: G Modal Tuning
(GDGCD)

     This very beautiful and archaic-sounding tuning consists of an open G chord lacking a third and with a suspended fourth added. The resulting sound is neither major nor minor, though it would strike most people as minor because of its open, melancholy character. It's particularly useful for poignant melodies like "Shady Grove", "The Cuckoo", and many of the old ballads. Some of the old timers refer to this tuning as "sawmill" or "mountain minor" tuning. Some tunes sound interesting with the fifth string tuned down to F.

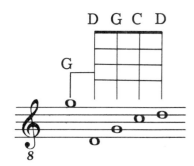

Banjo: G Modal Tuning

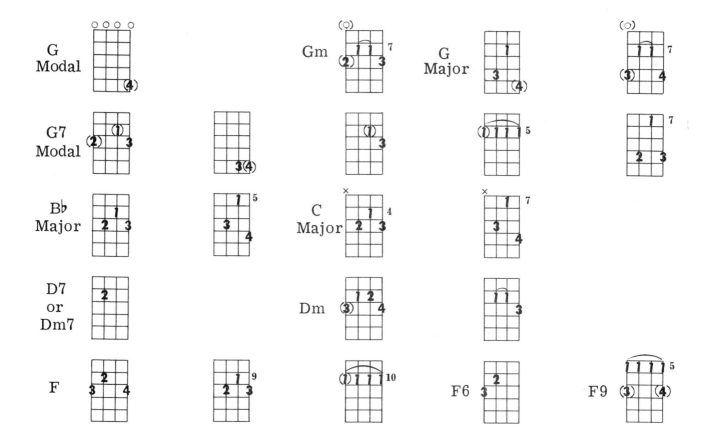

The banjo is not tuned to an open chord, but rather open G tuning is adapted in order to facilitate playing in the key of C by lowering the fourth string a whole tone from D to C:

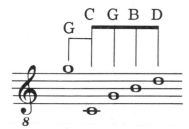

Standard C is rarely used in bluegrass, but is in wide use for other traditional and contemporary music, especially for playing fiddle tunes. It works well for both C and C minor, and the key of A minor (fifth string returned to A) is also easily accessible. This tuning has a very bright sound, and is especially useful for melodies that lie too low to be expressed effectively in any of the G tunings. Some tunes in C sound interesting with the fifth string retuned to E or even D. A few players like to retune the whole banjo one tone higher (to AD AC♯E) in order to accompany fiddlers in the favorite fiddle key of D without using a capo. If you do this, remember to name the chords in the following diagrams one tone higher (e.g. C becomes D, G7 becomes A7, etc.).

This tuning is also the standard tuning for the plectrum banjo, an instrument which is hardly played anymore. It is like a five-string banjo, but without the fifth string.

During the nineteenth century the standard tuning for banjo was an A tuning, exactly like this one, with the strings tuned in equivalent relationships but three frets (a minor third) lower: EAEG♯B. Old ragtime and minstrel sheet music arrangements are difficult or impossible to play in any other tuning.

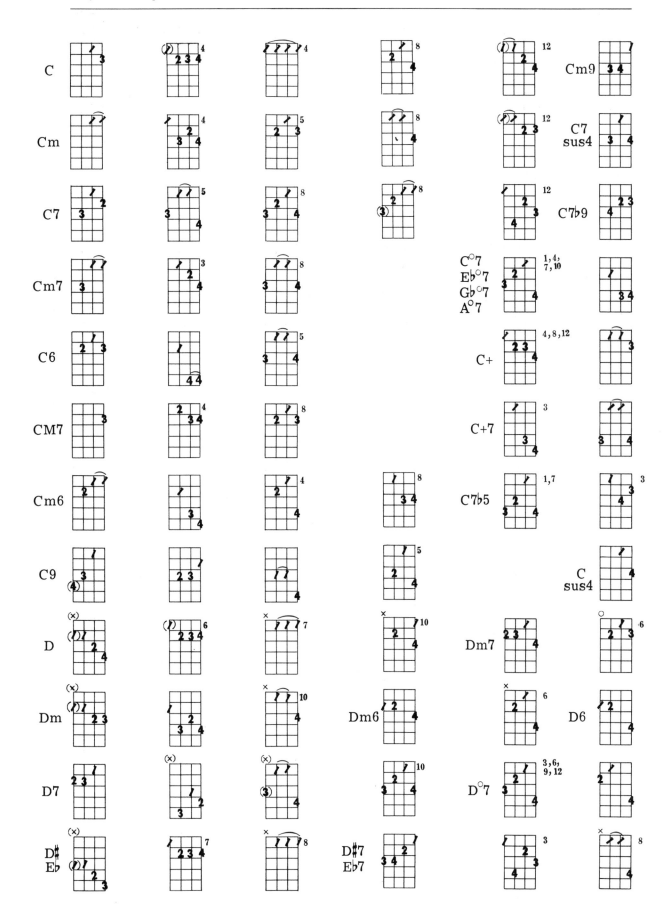

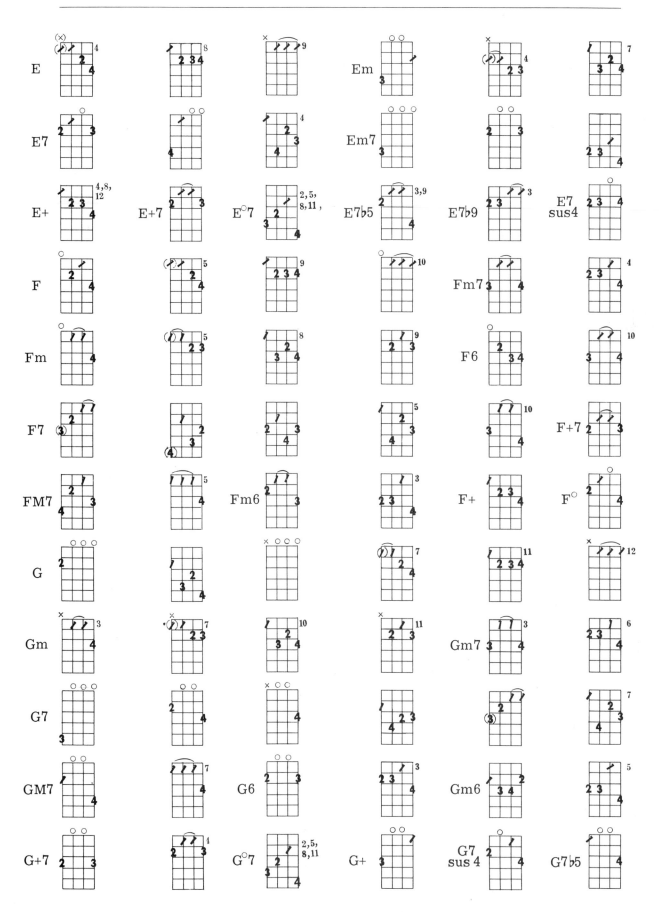

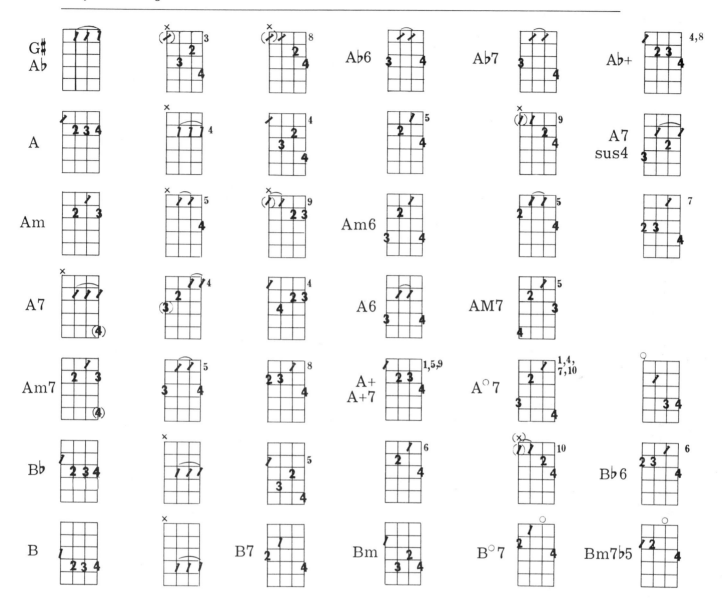

Banjo: Open C Tuning
(GCGCE)

In this tuning the banjo is tuned to an open C chord:

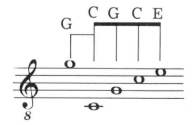

This tuning is used more often by ''contemporary'' than by ''mountain'' players. It offers certain possibilities, particularly in the way of ''bluesy'' sounds, that are less readily achieved in standard C tuning. Some interesting fifth-string tuning variations are E and D.

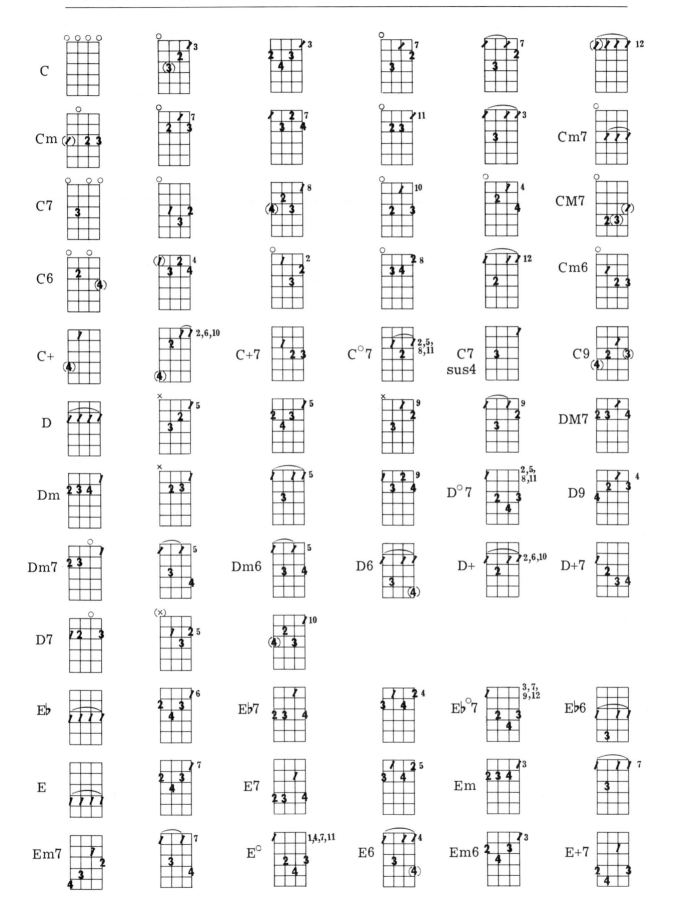

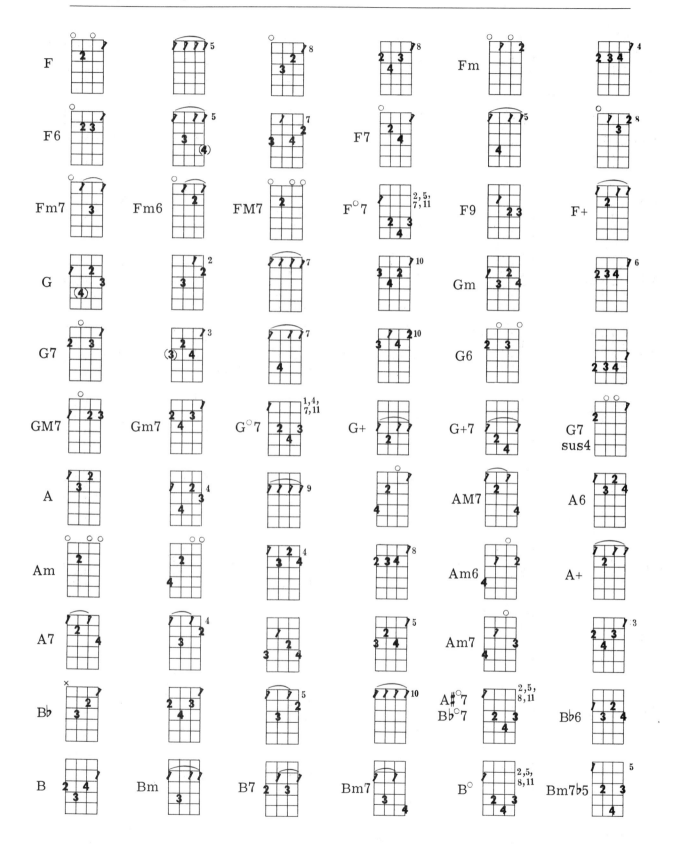

Banjo: Open C Minor Tuning
(GCGCE♭)

In this tuning the banjo is tuned to an open C minor chord:

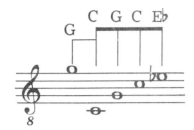

This tuning is rarely found in traditional or bluegrass music, but is often used by contemporary players for modern tunes, or to give an original twist to an old tune. It is especially useful for melodies that lie too low in range to be expressed effectively in any of the G tunings.

Banjo: Open C Minor Tuning

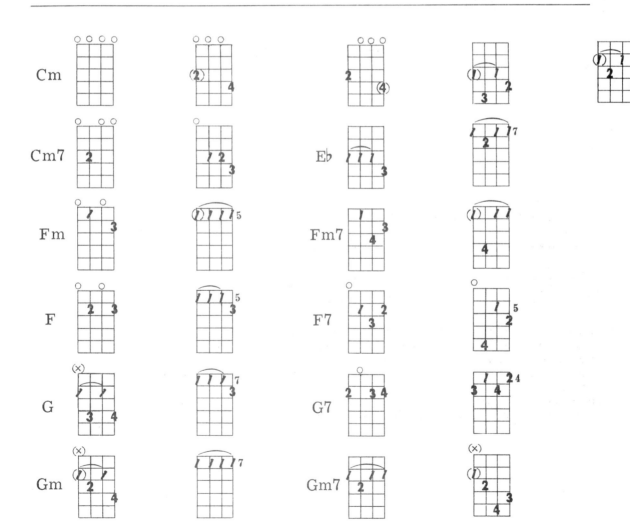

**Banjo: Old-Time C Tuning
(GCGCD)**

The banjo is not tuned to an open chord in this tuning, which lies half-way between the standard C and open C tunings. The resulting intervals lend themselves particularly well to expressing the melodies of many fiddle tunes. Since fiddlers prefer to play these tunes in D, this tuning is very commonly used with the capo on the second fret and the fifth string tuned up to A. Some tunes sound good with the fifth string tuned to E (F♯ with capo).

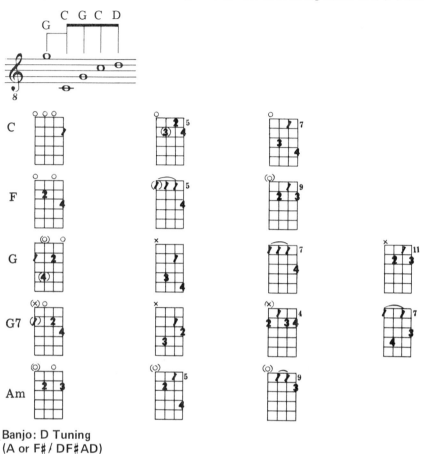

**Banjo: D Tuning
(A or F♯ / DF♯AD)**

In this tuning the banjo is tuned to an open D chord:

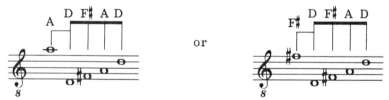

This is an extremely common tuning for traditional and bluegrass tunes with a low melodic range, and it offers a much darker sound than G tuning. You have to make your own decision in the case of each individual song about whether to tune the fifth string to F♯ or A. In general, A offers more versatility in the way it sounds with the other chords you're most likely to use.

D tuning can also be used effectively to play in the key of G, with the fifth string tuned to G, or in the key of E minor with the fifth string tuned to E.

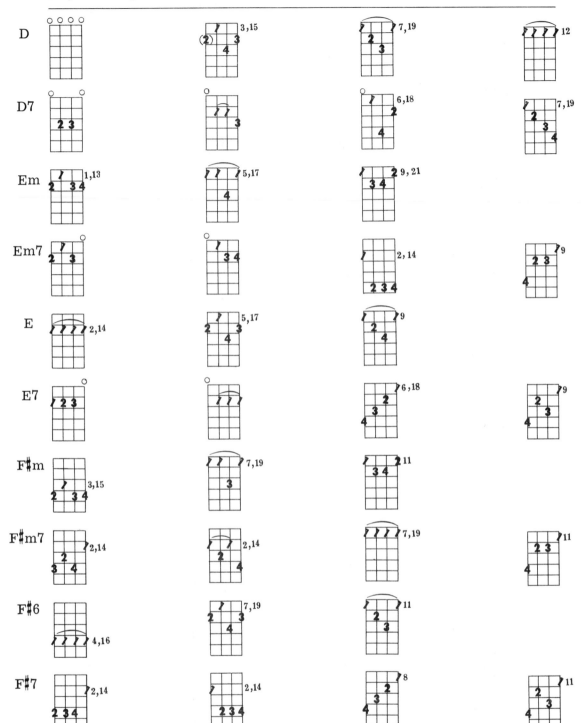

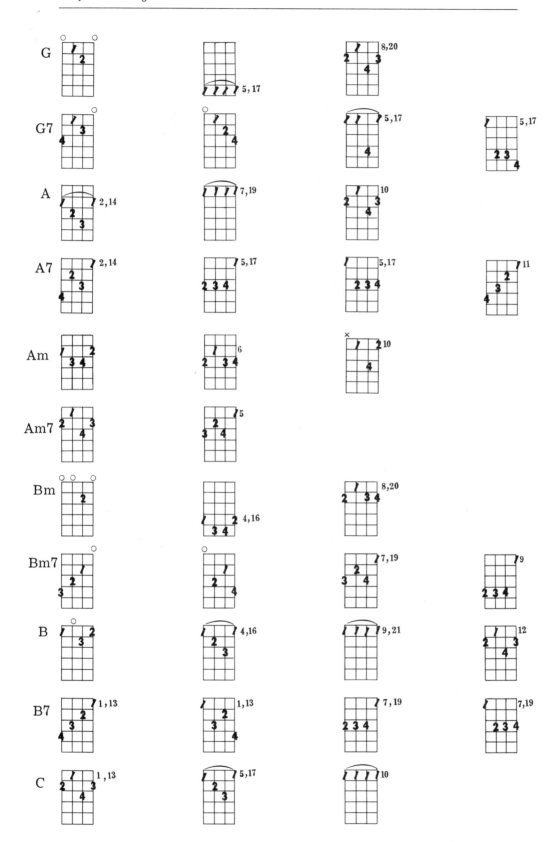

Fiddle Tunings

In addition to the standard violin tuning, numerous other tunings are used in American fiddle music, in order to gain access to the drones, double-stops and unisons that give certain tunes in certain keys their characteristic sounds.

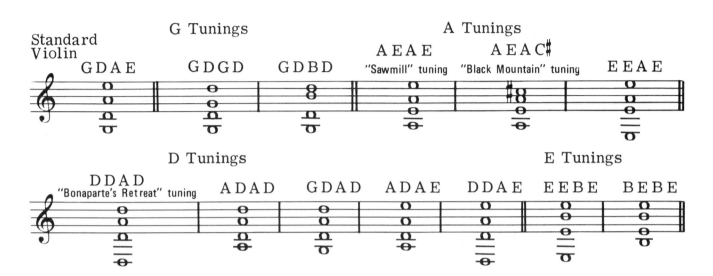

Tunings for Mandolin, Mandola, Mando-Cello and Tenor Banjo

The mandolin has four pairs of strings tuned GG DD AA EE — in other words, like a double-strung violin. Occasionally a mandolin player will use one of the fiddle tunings listed above.

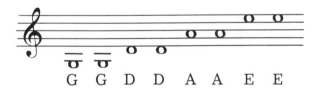

The tenor banjo has four single strings tuned to relatively equivalent intervals five tones lower than the mandolin: C G D A. The mandola is tuned the same, the mando-cello an octave lower. (The mando-cello may also be tuned an octave lower than the mandolin, or to the first four strings of a guitar, or to a five-string banjo tuning.)

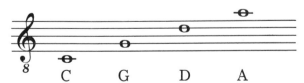

Some of the chord diagrams in this section require a stretch of an extra fret beyond the length of the diagram. These "missing" frets are indicated by the fret numbers to the right of the diagram. Some of these chords are intended only for the short fingerboard of the mandolin, and are difficult or impossible on the larger scale of the tenor banjo, mandola, etc.

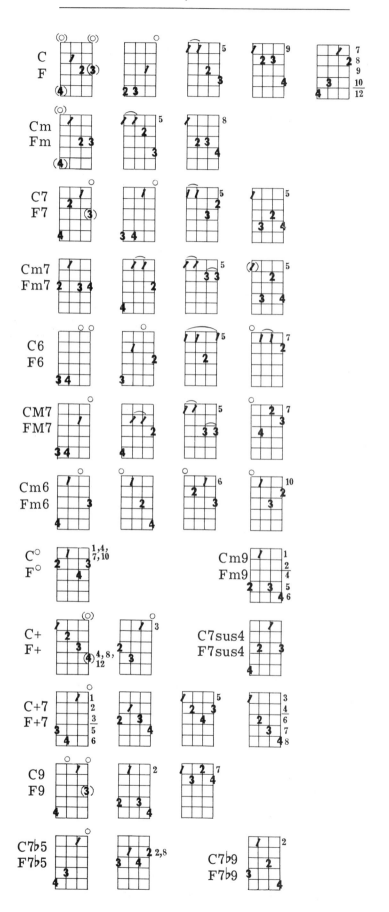

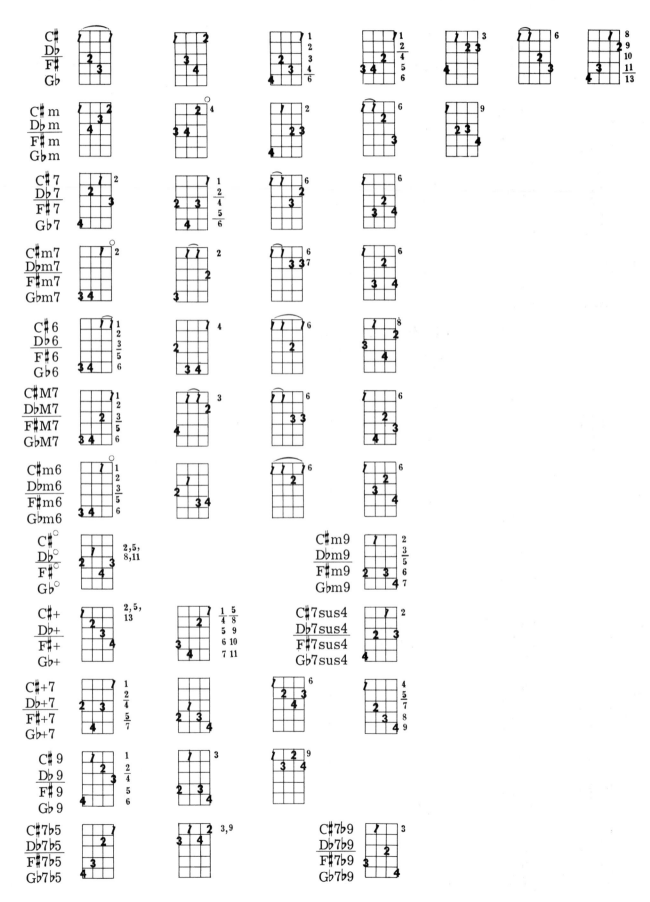

62

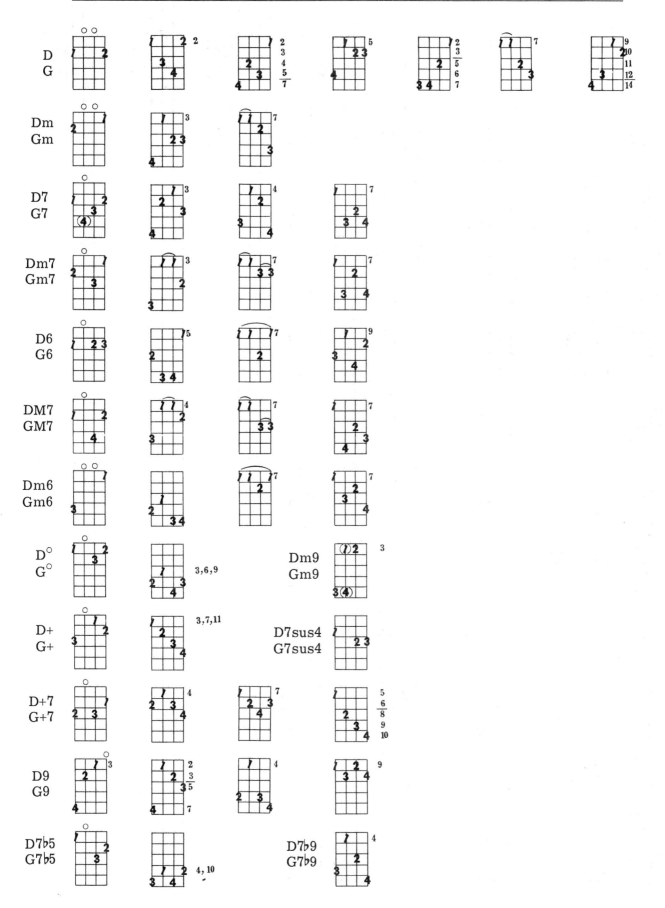

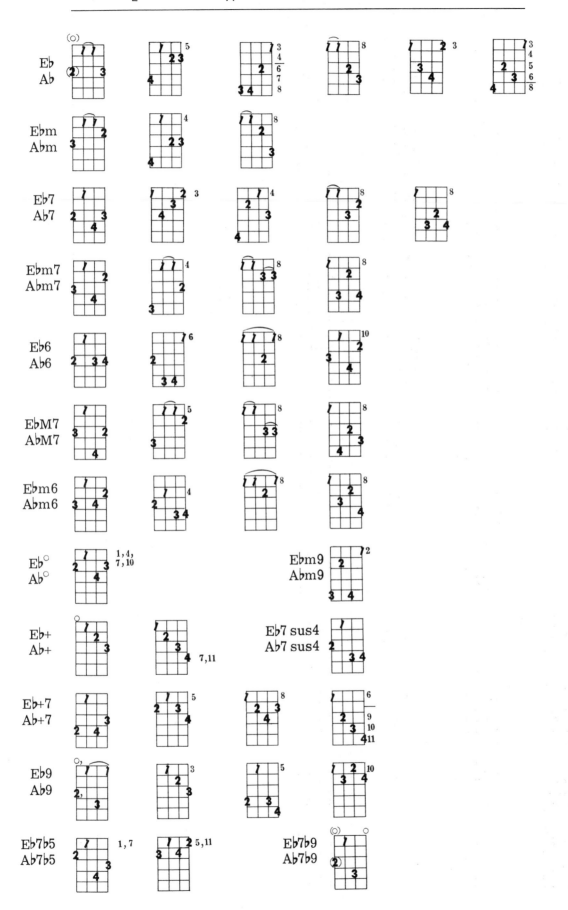

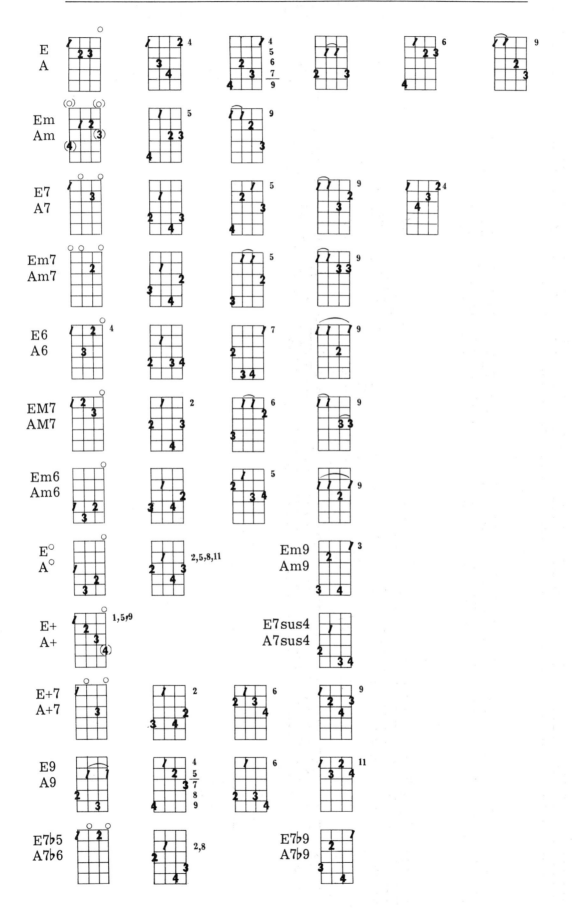

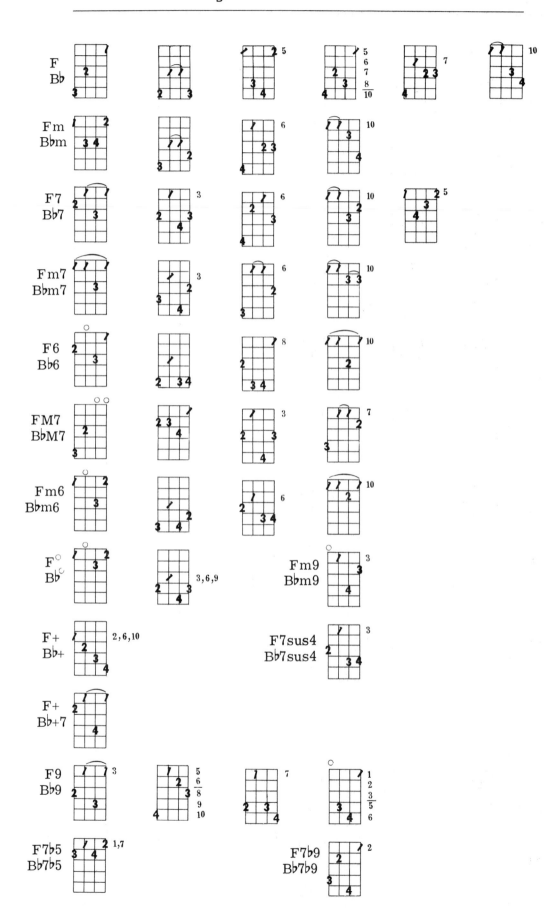

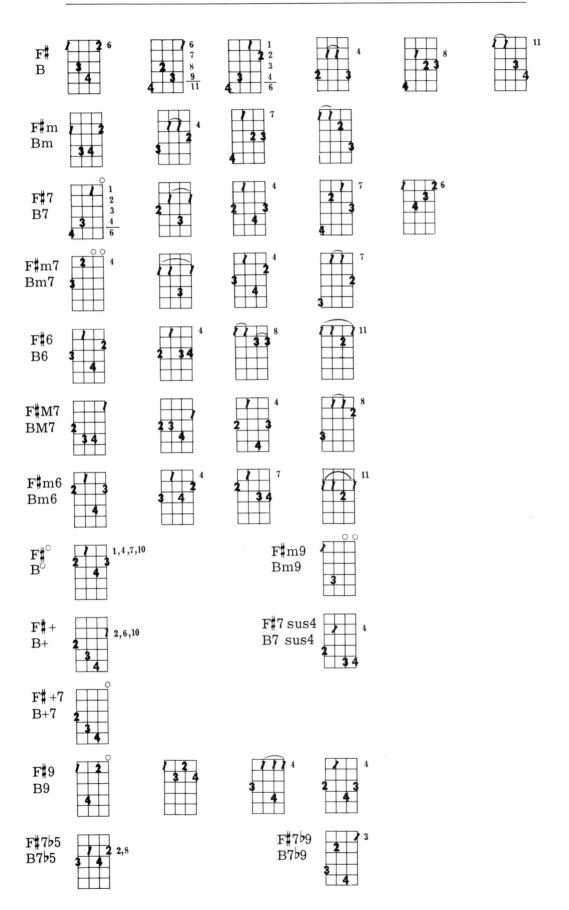

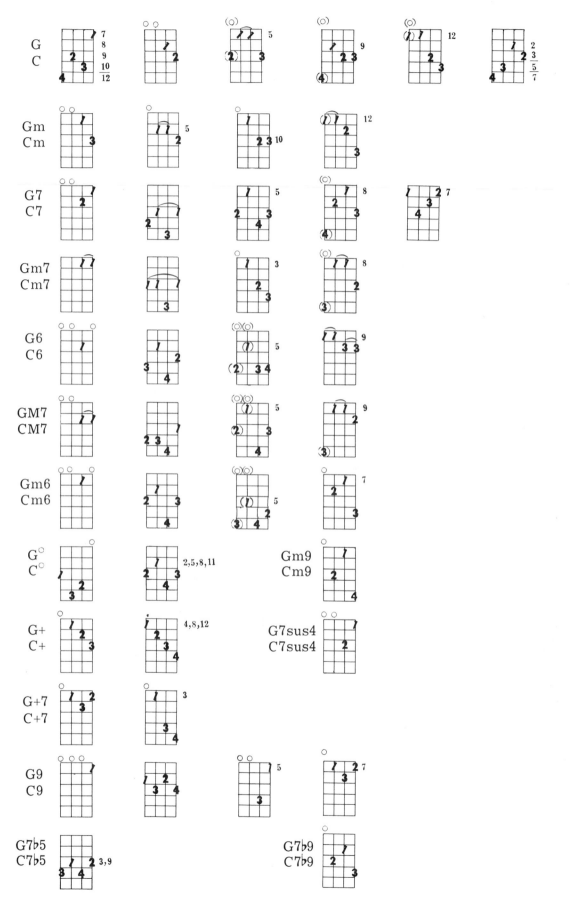

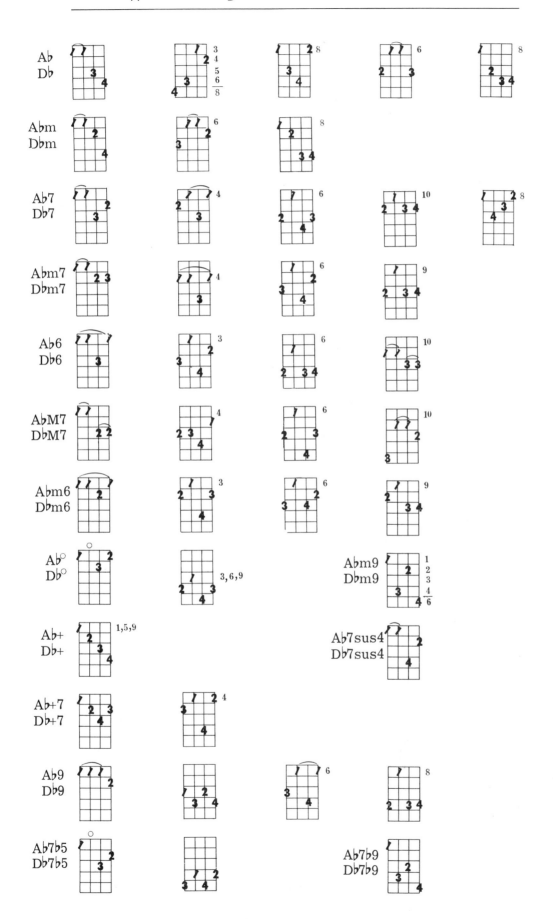

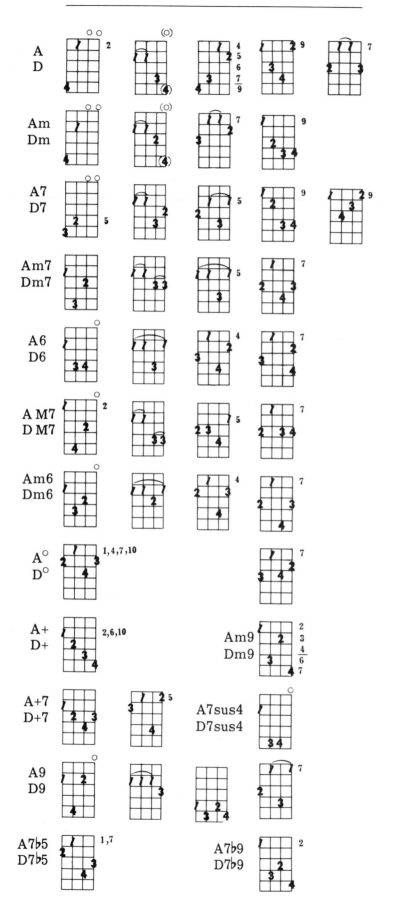

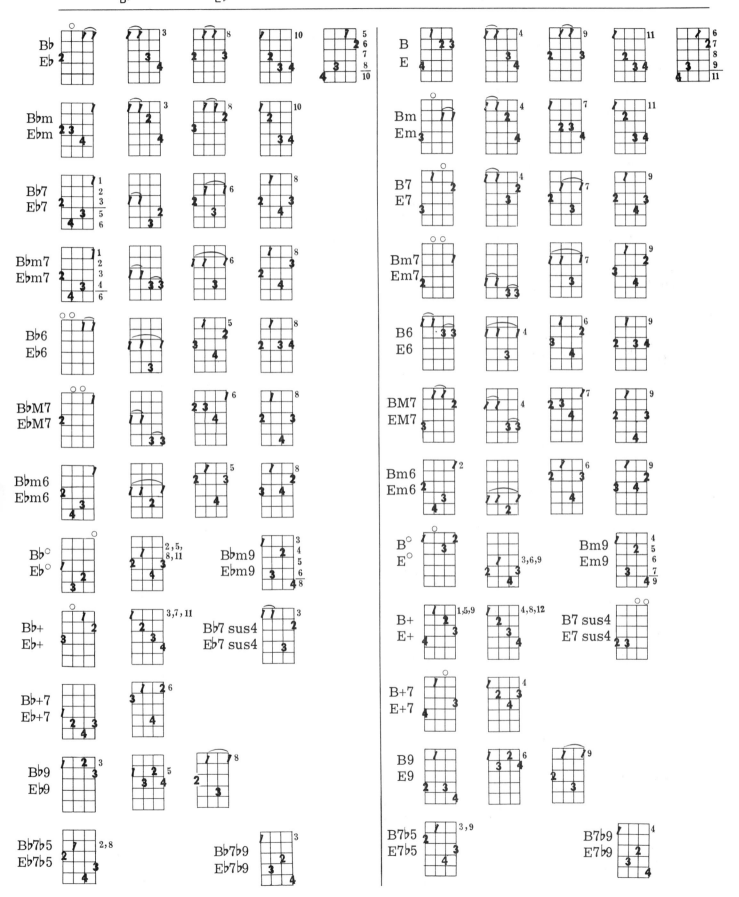